**Praise for *I Had a Miscarriage: A Memoir, a Movement***

"Zucker delivers an illuminating discussion of miscarriage in her strikingly intimate debut memoir."
      —*PUBLISHERS WEEKLY* (starred review)

"A contemplative, sensitive, and necessary work in the field of pregnancy and parenting."
      —*KIRKUS REVIEWS*

"Zucker asks her readers to take what they know about grief and pregnancy loss and turn it on its head, to reject the social norms. This takes practice and thoughtful risk-taking. But something has to change. Zucker's memoir is the first step."
      —*THE RUMPUS*

"Jessica Zucker's work—in her clinical practice, her online community, and now this powerful book—gives people permission to acknowledge their loss and process their grief. This totally absorbing memoir will reduce the isolation that so many who experience pregnancy loss feel. It's about time."
      —**GABRIELLE BIRKNER**, coauthor of *Modern Loss: Candid Conversation about Grief. Beginners Welcome.*

"Millions of women experience miscarriages every year. Why, then, is a miscarriage still a loss that our culture views as less extreme and less irretrievable than any other kind of gutting loss? *I Had a Miscarriage* by Jessica Zucker knocks down this ridiculous ladder of loss. Rooted in her knowledge as a specialist in reproductive and maternal mental health, this book creates a space for women to speak, to grieve, and to live alongside their loss instead of being expected to 'just get over it.' This book is a gift."
      —**EMILY RAPP BLACK**, author of *The Still Point of the Turning World*

"This gripping book should rest in the hands of every woman around the world, most especially those who have experienced pregnancy loss. It serves as an immeasurably helpful guide in a

time when vital support is needed—and often can't be found. Providing a sense of connection, this story reiterates that there is always community behind us."

—**CHRISTY TURLINGTON BURNS**, founder of Every Mother Counts

"As a husband who held his wife while she experienced a second-trimester miscarriage, I appreciated the depths Jessica Zucker was willing to explore in order to share her remarkable story and to generate awareness about this type of devastating loss. *I Had a Miscarriage* is a poignant book that both men and women can benefit from in order to process the grief of a miscarriage."

—**DAN CRANE**, journalist, author, and documentary filmmaker

"Miscarriage is a common occurrence in our society, but we rarely discuss it. Instead, we pretend that people around the world aren't miscarrying every day and that our cultural silence around their loss isn't keeping them silent about their pain. Jessica Zucker's powerful book brings their stories out of the shadows, exploring how we've created a society that doesn't understand how to address the pain of miscarriage and therefore ignores it. *I Had a Miscarriage* is an honest, vulnerable, and important account of a societal issue that will never go away, and encourages us to figure out how to address a pain that should weigh on all of us."

—**EVETTE DIONNE**, editor in chief of Bitch Media

"*I Had a Miscarriage* masterfully dismantles the shame and stigma heaped upon reproductive health issues, mental health treatment, and speaking out about taboo topics. We all know people who have had miscarriages; we all know the trauma and silence that shrouds this loss. This, too, is a reproductive justice issue. We must tell our stories. Thank you, Dr. Zucker."

—**SARAH SOPHIE FLICKER**, artist and activist

"The book I wish I had with me on my topsy-turvy road to motherhood."

—**PIERA GELARDI,** cofounder of Refinery29

"By writing so bravely and candidly about her own miscarriage, Dr. Zucker has given us a deeply humane book, inviting conversation and community into what for many has been a place of shame and silence. This is a book for everyone whose life has been touched by the loss of a pregnancy."

—**CAROL GILLIGAN**, author of *In a Different Voice*

"Dr. Zucker's book compassionately shows that there is no one way to grieve a miscarriage, and in doing so normalizes a spectrum of mourning we don't talk about nearly enough. There are lessons on grief for all of us—whether we have experienced miscarriage or not—in her brilliant, beautiful pages. A must read."

—**LORI GOTTLIEB**, author of *Maybe You Should Talk to Someone*

"When my pregnancy suddenly and painfully ended, Dr. Zucker's #IHadaMiscarriage campaign gave me a lifeline and a silent virtual community of witnesses and words when I had none. Documenting her experience with this riveting memoir helps us all normalize miscarriage experiences and end stigma, shame, and silence."

—**YAMANI HERNANDEZ**, executive director of the National Network of Abortion Funds

"*I Had a Miscarriage* provides the badly needed space to share, grieve, and unpack pregnancy loss. Dr. Jessica Zucker paints a nuanced and frank portrait of the many different ways miscarriage is experienced, and in that portrait, she educates and illuminates—and comforts, too. This book is a solace and a rallying call for change. Let us speak openly and honestly about that which affects so many of us. I am grateful for this book."

—**EDAN LEPUCKI**, author of *California*

"An essential book for those raw in grief or looking to support and understand a loved one's sorrow. This is a compassionate love story about death and life, written by an expert who not only counsels but also has experienced such harrowing loss. Zucker's warmth, insight, and honesty make every page bloom with tenderness."

—**MIRA PTACIN**, author of *Poor Your Soul*

"The book you need that you wish you didn't. Jessica Zucker is an expert in pregnancy loss who's lived it too, and she delivers a much-needed call for new ways to acknowledge, grieve, and gather around what has been an exclusively private pain for too long."

—**ANNA SALE**, author of *Let's Talk About Hard Things*

"This powerful and important book is for men as much as for women. By breaking the silence on lost pregnancies, Zucker throws a lifeline to grieving parents who should know that they're not alone and it's not their fault."

—**DAN SCHWERIN**, former senior advisor to Hillary Clinton

"*I Had a Miscarriage* is an incredible reflection on grief and resilience, lifting the veil on a topic so often mired in shame. Kudos to Jessica Zucker for this necessary and moving book."

—**JESSICA VALENTI**, author of *Sex Object: A Memoir*

"For too long, those suffering from pregnancy loss have felt isolated and alone. In her moving and insightful memoir, Dr. Zucker shares her profound wisdom. Those who've endured pregnancy loss, or their friends and family, will find the stories shared in these compelling pages to be of great comfort. A necessary book."

—**ZEV WILLIAMS**, MD, PhD, chief of the Division of Reproductive Endocrinology and Infertility at Columbia University Medical Center

"Jessica Zucker's #IHadaMiscarriage campaign gave voice to the unspeakable reality of miscarriage; now, her book goes deeper to explore what she names the trifecta of silence, shame, and stigma women experience following a reproductive loss. Even identifying that miscarriage is a real loss, worthy of real grief, is radical in a society that denies this fact, and Zucker slyly laces her relatable personal story with this bold feminist argument. Her story is as wrenching as it is healing, and the narrative is made even richer by her expertise as a maternal mental health professional. Thus, we get raw storytelling alongside brilliant advice for helping ourselves, and those we love, grieve. It is a book that will mean a lot to so many people, and one I won't forget."

—**ALLISON YARROW**, author of *90s Bitch: Media, Culture, and the Failed Promise of Gender Equality*

# I HAD A MISCARRIAGE

## *A Memoir, a Movement*

...

## JESSICA ZUCKER, PhD

**THE FEMINIST PRESS**
AT THE CITY UNIVERSITY OF NEW YORK
**NEW YORK CITY**

Published in 2021 by the Feminist Press
at the City University of New York
The Graduate Center
365 Fifth Avenue, Suite 5406
New York, NY 10016

feministpress.org

First Feminist Press edition 2021

This book was made possible thanks to a grant from New York State
Council on the Arts with the support of Governor Andrew M. Cuomo and
the New York State Legislature.

This book is supported in part by an award from the National
Endowment for the Arts.

Second printing April 2021

Cover design by Samantha Hahn
Text design by Drew Stevens

**Library of Congress Cataloging-in-Publication Data**
Names: Zucker, Jessica, author.
Title: I had a miscarriage : a memoir, a movement / Jessica Zucker.
Description: First Feminist Press edition. | New York, NY : The Feminist
    Press at the City University of New York, 2021.
Identifiers: LCCN 2020029350 (print) | LCCN 2020029351 (ebook) | ISBN
    9781558612884 (paperback) | ISBN 9781558612891 (ebook)
Subjects: LCSH: Zucker, Jessica. | Miscarriage--Psychological aspects. |
    Pregnant women--United States--Biography. | Clinical
    psychologists--United States--Biography. | Parental grief.
Classification: LCC RG648 .Z83 2021 (print) | LCC RG648 (ebook) | DDC
    618.3/920651--dc23
LC record available at https://lccn.loc.gov/2020029350
LC ebook record available at https://lccn.loc.gov/2020029351

PRINTED IN THE UNITED STATES OF AMERICA

*For those who know this ache too well.*

*And of course,*
*for Olive.*

**Preface**

This, like nearly all stories about pregnancy and pregnancy loss, is really a story about motherhood. How we define it. How we arrive at it. If we do. And how we're impacted by it all.

There is no singular path to motherhood. We don't always become mothers through pregnancy. Maybe we do, through our own eggs, donor eggs, donor sperm, intra-uterine insemination (IUI), in vitro fertilization (IVF), or other methods. Or maybe we've fostered, adopted, or gone the surrogacy route. Some mothers have children teeming underfoot; others hold them in memory without tangible proof. There's childlessness, too. In conversations about pregnancy and loss, including in this book, it behooves us to look at the entire spectrum of pregnancies, births, and the myriad ways we become mothers.

There is no universal pregnancy experience, outcome, or emotional reaction. As each one of us navigates the unpredictable outcomes of the reproductive spectrum, we are often faced with the need to acknowledge or come to terms with our own emotional and/or physical edge that shapes the very aspects that are within our control. How long to try, how far to go, how much to endure—on a multitude of levels. Maybe we stop trying to get pregnant altogether. Maybe we never try at all. Either way, it's incumbent upon us to honor and respect the diversity of these situations, whether they are by choice or by circumstance. There are countless potential stumbling blocks: infertility, secondary infertility, not conceiving again after loss, health problems, medical complications, relational concerns, financial constraints related to insurance, reproductive technologies and family building, and so on.

The pregnancy/motherhood/loss community should aim to be inclusive of all experiences and all perspectives: miscarriage, early loss, later loss, recurrent loss, stillbirth, twin loss, termination for medical reasons, neonatal and infant loss, not getting pregnant in the first place, and others. All are profoundly important and all are a part of this story. And in here, all are welcome. As loss moms, we understand too well that pregnancy and the loss of it affects us and our families in complex ways. It can change us for good. I know it changed me.

And just as the variety of reproductive outcomes and their possible physical, mental, and emotional implications are honored here, so are the array of people who experience them. Throughout these pages, I will use "woman" or "women" to describe people who've experienced a miscarriage, stillbirth, infant loss, or infertility. This isn't because these losses only happen to cisgender women. One's gender does not dictate what reproductive outcomes one does or does not experience. Rather, as someone who identifies as a cis woman, and as a psychologist who predominately treats cis women, my use of "woman" is simply a way to remain true to my experience and those of my patients. It does not, in any way, erase the experience of trans, nonbinary, genderqueer, and two-spirit people, who—in addition to shouldering what can be a profound, long-lasting grief associated with pregnancy and infant loss—often have to endure discrimination within the medical community and elsewhere, the erasure of their gender identity, and exclusion from loss communities.

Miscarriage, pregnancy, and infant loss is not just a "woman's experience." It does not discriminate.

There is also no "one way" to feel about these specific losses, so while this book does primarily center around the grief and mourning that can and does reside in the wake of a miscarriage, I want to acknowledge and make space for the people who feel indifferent toward their pregnancy losses, or even relieved. Far too often, those who do not experience sadness or anger following a miscarriage, be it privately or publicly, are made to feel defective by a society that has long since demanded female bodies not only procreate but express a deep, innate desire to do so. But there is nothing broken about those who feel thankful for no longer being pregnant, just like there was nothing broken about those who wanted to carry a pregnancy to term, but couldn't. In these pages, all are welcome.

And I also want to acknowledge that my experience represents just that—my experience. Unlike far too many Black and brown women in this country, I do not face a higher rate of maternal mortality. In the throes of my loss, I did not face the fear of being unable to access the care I needed. I have, based on the color of my skin, benefited from white privilege. And while this privilege does not shield any of us from tragedy, including the loss of a pregnancy, it does protect us from the compounding tragedies incurred by systemic racism. It certainly protected me.

It is my desire to cultivate a space where we can all share our stories if and when we want and need to; a space where they can be honored in whatever way we see fit; a space of understanding, support, and continued healing. So as we wade through this transformational time in our lives, I encourage us to remember that we are all deserving of support. Free from grief hierarchies or timelines, we must be gentle with ourselves during this nascent period and resist comparing and contrasting our stories. Your ache, relief, despair, or indifference is uniquely yours. It is yours to navigate in any way you choose, through whatever feelings arise—be they sadness, anger, hopefulness, neutrality, helplessness, fear, or a mix of them all. Throughout, I earnestly urge you to remember that you did absolutely nothing wrong—nothing to deserve this procreative event. Certain areas of our lives are beyond our control, and reproduction is one of them. It can be difficult to wrap our heads around this reality; to come to terms with the fact that we have no answers or that the concrete answers we do get might confound us all the more. And so sometimes we blame ourselves in the absence of clarity, as we search for something to pinpoint; an anchor to keep us grounded as we weather the barrage of emotional responses. We look for reasons when, more often than not, there are none.

Resist hurling blame—it won't undo what is done. Pregnancy loss is not a disease that can be cured; it's not going anywhere—it is, in fact, a normative outcome of pregnancy. And it is therefore a topic we would benefit from engaging in candidly and integrating into everyday conversations, devoid of silence, stigma, and shame. To help ourselves and to help future generations. To normalize the experience, its aftermath, and the grief that flows from it. To allow those of us who have gone through it to be simultaneously vulnerable about our circumstances and lovingly embraced for it.

Wherever you are in your journey, you deserve abounding support. And I hope you will find it in these pages. I am honored to share my story (and those of others) with you in the hope of underscoring and illuminating that you are not alone. Millions of people know this complexity, this pain. We have one another. Support is available for you. I hope you find it here.

# 1

*"I thought I was out of the woods."*

I was thirty-nine years old, living in Laurel Canyon, tucked in the hills of Hollywood, adjusting to life with a three-and-a-half-year-old, and had only recently coalesced with the idea of having a second child when I found out I was pregnant again.

I was nervous about having another child. The anticipated juggle felt daunting, but ultimately, after taking stock of my life and that of my family's, I landed on: doable. I began preparing—pulling dusty nursery gear out of the garage and sifting through newborn onesies our son had grown out of by his seventh week, some half-chewed wooden toys, and a jungle-themed mobile I remember tearing up over when I first unwrapped it four years earlier.

My husband and I started preparing in other, more nuanced, heady ways as well. The mechanics of prepping our home for another human being were relatively simple, but what proved to be even more demanding was the work of readying our minds for this significant transition: going from one kid to two seemed like way more than the sum of its parts. We mulled over the intricate details of life with two children: How would we negotiate our time? How would we manage Jason's extensive travel schedule for work? How could this shift potentially affect our respective work/life goals? We have always been the kind of parents who aimed to share the emotional labor of child-rearing as equally as we could; our marriage was built on a mutual respect of each other's strengths. He excels at all things creative, inventive, and playful, which translates into him being a joyful, grounded, and loving father and partner. I envisioned that his warmth and joie de vivre would only flourish with more members of our family, which encouraged us to throw caution to the wind—we were sure we would figure out the logistics somehow. It became a favorite hobby to daydream aloud about how our son would take to his newfound big-brother status, and how the growth of our little family would exponentially expand the love within it. Jointly, we decided it was wise to wait to share the pregnancy news with our son—given his age and his perception of time (or lack thereof)—until my baby bump was too obvious to ignore.

...

Preparing myself at work was another story entirely. I am a psychologist who specializes in reproductive and maternal mental health. The reality of my job means that pregnancy is almost always at the top of my mind, though not usually the media version that features glowing bellies and radiant mothers-to-be. In my office, I have instead heard countless heartbreaking stories from women struggling to get pregnant, coping with perinatal anxiety, grieving miscarriages, contemplating terminating pregnancies, selectively reducing multiples, and weathering postpartum mood and anxiety disorders. I speak to women who give birth to babies born silent, left with photos of their dead babies held ever so briefly, and those wrestling with taking ailing newborns off life support. I am with them during some of the most tragic moments imaginable. I listen as these women wonder if it'll ever be possible to put the pieces of their lives back together after all the wreckage.

Though hard to imagine at the time of my second pregnancy, I was in my fifth year of practice, and as much as one could be, I had grown accustomed to hearing about these situations. After all, I had heard them all while pregnant with my son too. During that nine-month period, I found I had little trouble psychologically separating myself from the pain and risk that comes with pregnancy. Naivete, maybe? Hearty denial, perhaps? But somehow, pregnant for a second time, I felt their stories differently, more acutely aware of the inherent risks that come along with this significant undertaking.

...

The early days of this second pregnancy ticked by mostly without event. I broke out my maternity jeans—though slightly earlier than I had with my first pregnancy. Soon, I spent nights tossing and turning with nausea and those initial hints of heartburn. By week seven or eight, I pretty much felt seasick around the clock. Compared to my experience with my son, this pregnancy was a trial in terms of just how ill I could possibly feel on any given day. A small part of me gnawed with wonder about the health of this pregnancy, based on nothing more than how horrid I felt because of it. I tried to reassure myself by thinking about an old wives' tale, which presupposes that the sicker you are, the more viable the pregnancy. In part because of my continued uneasiness, I was on edge awaiting the day I could receive the results of my forthcoming eighteen-week amniocentesis, an extensive prenatal diagnostic test that analyzes amniotic fluid for genetic conditions, chromosomal abnormalities, and neural tube defects.

Two weeks before I was to undergo the test—at sixteen-weeks pregnant—I went to the bathroom in my dermatologist's office on what should have been a standard Tuesday morning, wiped, and found cherry-red blood on the toilet paper. Seeing brownish blood discharged during pregnancy can be normal—a sign that old blood, previously stored up, is making way for new blood, vibrant and full of life. But this was different. I knew this was different. And I was alarmed beyond words at the sight of it: *I'm not supposed to menstruate while pregnant. This can't be normal. It just can't be.* Alone in that pink-tiled public bathroom, minutes from having a routine mole check, a wave of dread enveloped me as I frantically reached out to my ob-gyn. "There's blood!" Her calm but pointed reply included the litany of requisite questions:

"Did you exercise?"

"No."

"Did you have sex?" she asked plainly.

"NO!"

"Did you do anything differently than usual?"

"NO!" The panic rose in my voice.

My dermatologist remained calm as she sent me on my way to my obstetrician. I went straight from her office to my ob-gyn's to investigate. She broke out the ultrasound machine and we saw a strong heartbeat. The placenta was perfectly situated, everything sounded normal, fluid levels were as they should be. And so, I went on my way, reassured medically, though not emotionally.

...

On Wednesday morning, I felt well enough to head to work. My doctor advised me to do whatever felt best, and so I showered, dressed, added a pad to my underwear just in case, and arrived at my office. I was cautiously optimistic that the day would go smoothly and the crimson-red blood that had sent me into a panic wouldn't show itself again. I was calm and focused, and somehow mustered a sense of ease as I faced a full slate of patients.

Surprisingly, the day was okay. I got through it and, for the most part, felt good. But on my drive home, my uterus began to tighten intermittently. Like the tentacles of an octopus, strangulating discomfort enwrapped me, dissipating almost as quickly as the feelings arose. I called my dad, a doctor.

"Is it possible to have Braxton-Hicks contractions at sixteen weeks?" I asked.

"I suppose it's possible," he replied calmly.

But I knew. I knew these symptoms couldn't be typical. Even though they were *possible* at sixteen weeks, I knew deep down I wasn't going to make it to week forty.

Once I got home from work, I changed into loose-fitting clothes and sprawled out on my bed, vexed both in body and mind.

Later that evening, as the cramping worsened, I asked

my friend, who is a midwife, to come over and investigate my unexplained spotting, or at the very least, to check the baby's heartbeat one more time. I was desperate for information. Insight. Answers. By phone, she suggested I have a sip of red wine to reduce the cramping and take a warm bath, then quickly drove over to our house to listen in on the baby.

The sound emanating from the doppler reassured us yet again that everything was proceeding as it should: baby's heartbeat was as strong as ever. This brought a momentary sigh of relief, though the cramping continued, and my mind barked a cacophonous chaos of what-ifs. I tried hard to quell these grave thoughts. I had to. There was nothing I could do to change whatever course this pregnancy was already on, and there was no way to know why these things were happening or what was wrong. So we popped in a movie for some much-needed distraction, and I tried to lose myself in a narrative that wasn't my own. I tried to find rest in those less intense moments when the cramping slowed but my mind could not.

It was a futile effort. I was up most of the night, roiling in thought-stopping physical torment. For ten-plus hours, I was trying to ward off—or somehow make peace with—the ebb and flow of the pain. Some moments were so intense, though, I felt like the wind was knocked straight out of me. Unable to speak, unable to catch my breath. The spotting, at this point, was an unconvincing shade of dull red, which seemed like a positive development, but still, I was unsure of how anxious I should be. I reminded myself of the encouraging doctor's appointment throughout my sleepless night. There was no indication whatsoever that death was lurking on the horizon.

When things hadn't improved by Thursday morning, my headspace plummeted, and the worry I had attempted to stave off not only resurfaced, but multiplied. Because of my sleepless night, I asked my husband to manage our son's morning routine. The fact that my pain level was too severe for me to be involved was concerning to my husband. But he, like I, was not fully prepared to face the ramifications of any outcome other than the one that would end five months from that moment with us bringing home our second baby. He, like I, hoped this tornado of pain, uncertainty, and emotional overwhelm was temporary.

Still, I called a friend to ask if she'd be able to take our son, Liev, home from preschool at the end of the day and keep him for a while, just in case I still felt like this in the late afternoon. My husband was incredulous: "Why would this random Thursday be the time for our child's first-ever sleepover? Isn't he still too young for that?" The answer was probably yes, he wasn't quite ready for a sleepover, but neither would he be prepared to see trauma unfurl before his fledgling eyes. While I couldn't have anticipated in my wildest dreams (nightmares, more like) what was about to happen, I still didn't want to take the chance that my sweet boy would have to witness anything grim.

The last thing I wanted was to be alone, but I didn't ask Jason to stay either. He had an important workday ahead, and I figured I'd be uncomfortable at best and unable to play cars with my son in the afternoon at worst. So my husband left for work, my son for school, and there I was. Alone.

And that was when I realized there was no going back. There would be no going back to unbuttoning my jeans after a meal to make room for my growing belly. No going back to joking about how badly I wanted a beer with dinner—a hoppy IPA I could almost taste even though I was entering my fifth month without one.

Then, there would be *nothing but* going back. Back in time. Losing the pregnancy, and becoming a mother of one again. I miscarried, in my home.

• • •

As the cramps strengthened through the morning hours and the color of the blood changed from dull to bright once again, I began to pull my pants on to go see the perinatologist. I hoped seeing this maternal-fetal expert, a subspecialist of obstetrics who performs the twenty-week anatomy scans, genetic amniocentesis, and other such procedures concerning fetal care, would give me answers, even though it was unlikely he'd have any additional information than what I had ascertained two days prior at my ob-gyn's. But I was desperate. I was determined. I was obsessed with finding a way, any way, to keep a tight grip on a future that, on some level, I knew was slipping away.

I never made it to his office that afternoon. As I shimmied myself into one of my maternity tops, panic overtook me. My palms began to sweat, my heart raced as if I'd just run a half marathon or downed gallons of undiluted black coffee. I felt light-headed and sure I'd lose consciousness. Somehow, I made it to the bathroom, shuffling slowly. I thought if I could simply empty my bladder, calm my breath and apply a cold compress to my face, I would resume normalcy.

Breathe.

I didn't know it then, but I was in the active phase of childbirth, in what is termed "transition." Moments from expelling a baby, the body rejiggers for release.

...

I heard a pop. Or did I? For better or worse, I simply do not know anymore. Maybe there was a distinct sound; a warning, as if my body was trying to say, "Please, get ready." Perhaps there wasn't, but in the recesses of my mind I have created an audible line in the sands of time that distinguishes the "before" and the "after." Before and after I felt an urge, almost a compulsion, to howl a guttural "no" in sheer and utter disbelief. Before and after I looked down. Before and after I saw her.

When I started to urinate, something I to this day have trouble even recalling occurred. Something that would change me in ways both diminutive and profound. Something that, unlike the "pop" that may or may not have occurred, I cannot force my mind to question. My baby slid out. I saw her there, dead, dangling from me mere inches from the toilet-bowl water. There was some movement—maybe just from falling? I don't and will never know—and, just like that, I was overcome with physical relief, after having labored for hours. A relief that anyone who's experienced childbirth will understand: the quick kind that's instantly replaced with an overwhelming gravity. My window-clad house should have shattered from the pitch of my prolonged primordial scream. It didn't.

I did.

...

I frantically texted my doctor; somehow I had the presence of mind to know that if I didn't, not only would my daughter die, but so could I. She called immediately. I was loud, clamoring for instructions on how to handle the medical chaos.

Her first direction was to get a pair of scissors. *Scissors!* I walked from the toilet to the medicine cabinet for a pair that had previously only been called to duty for eyebrow trimming. I reached down and held the baby, clutching her close to my vagina, which was all the umbilical cord would allow. I knew I had to get back to the toilet to make the cut—to be near the phone and my doctor's counsel; to spare my hardwood floors. One can't explain the places our brains go in these moments. Nothing can prepare us for these confounding traumas—*nothing*—so I try to grant myself the grace that comes with knowing I survived as best I could. I cared about the hardwood floors, because some part of me knew my mind could not focus on much more.

I crouched over the toilet and cut the umbilical cord, then immediately began to bleed in an obviously emergent way. She was in my hands ever so briefly. She. But as the medical emergency I knew I was experiencing grew more dire, I placed her on a nearby hand towel. No longer part of a symbiotic union, dizzy with despair and confusion over this separation, I somehow found a way to stay the course on the practical matters of caring for myself: attempting to get dressed, stuffing towels into my underwear because the hemorrhaging wouldn't stop until the placenta was delivered. My doctor talked me through what to do, stressing the need to get to her office, and quickly, with my baby in a bag to send to the lab for testing.

I wish I had had it in me to spend more time with her connected to me, before the cutting and the bleeding and the primal rush to save my own life; before the hand towel and the completely incongruous plastic grocery bag. But it didn't feel possible. Things were moving fast. My heartbeat. My doctor's words. The blood.

Alone with her in my bathroom—the bathroom where I had envisioned giving her a first bath, or watching her and her older brother splash playfully in the tub—I continued to flush the toilet over and over as the bowl refilled with my blood. This was an emergency situation, but I knew if I called 911, I'd have to somehow make it down four flights of stairs, including ones outside, to let the paramedics in. I couldn't manage it, nor did I really want a group of strangers running through my home in the midst of this intimate collapse of my life.

And there she was. She. She was bigger than I would've expected at sixteen weeks along. She seemed robust. She seemed possible. In her face, I saw such a clear resemblance to my sweet little Liev, my son who had just been robbed of a sibling.

My doctor insisted I stay on the phone with her until Jason arrived, as he darted through Hollywood traffic to get to me. He ignored red lights and stop signs, but still needed to weave up jam-packed Laurel Canyon Boulevard. I had texted him in the late morning with an update about the change in hue and intensity of the blood, and so when the baby emerged there on the toilet, I texted again in earnest. "The baby fell out. I need you. Please come home," I wrote as my hands shook. (On that particular day, he was working in close quarters with colleagues, hence the texting instead of calling.)

An eeriness set in after the initial rush of adrenaline—a surreal, documentary-like feel. My mind slowed. This level of intensity was something I had only seen in movies, I thought, and was aware that I could either die here or summon the fortitude to push on.

• • •

The truth is, at sixteen weeks pregnant, I had thought I was out of the woods. I assumed braving the first trimester and making it into the second meant I was in the safe zone, where pregnancies stuck and fetuses were bound to become babies. Somewhere around eight or nine weeks, I shared the news of my pregnancy with family and friends. I wasn't necessarily a proponent of waiting until the second trimester, as our culture tends to advocate, but I'll admit, a tiny part of me was concerned that sharing my news early might somehow jinx it. I had long figured that if I were to miscarry, I would surely want my cadre of loved ones in the know, tucked in by my side and supporting me.

My belly bulged, prompting patients to ask about my current state of affairs. "Yes, I'm pregnant," I'd reply. "Due in the spring, early April." I'd answered the standard gamut of questions: "How are you feeling?" (Like crap, mostly.) "What are you having?" (A girl. This time we found out the sex, unlike my pregnancy with Liev, in which we decided to keep that a surprise.) I suddenly realized I had a lot of people to reach out to when catastrophe struck.

Sitting there on the toilet, in an effort to galvanize physical and emotional wherewithal, I fervently texted a few of my closest friends and family "I HAD A MISCARRIAGE." I could not summon them to physically be by my side, but as the blood continued to drain from my body and she remained in my presence—both of and not of this world—I found myself reaching for some semblance of community, of comfort, of a way to tether myself to the living as I remained in the presence of death.

In the meantime, Jason had made it home, and I had instructions to relay to him from the doctor, who was still on the phone.

"Get a plastic bag!" I shouted. "Put her in it so we can bring her to Dr. Schneider's office." Anything but grounded, reeling from his own experience of this trauma, he shot back, "Why are you calling it 'her'?!" before descending the three flights down to our kitchen, where leftover grocery bags were stored.

The last thing I needed was to hear him call the baby— *our* baby—"it." I don't know what I expected his reaction to be, but even in the very initial moments of my grief, I knew it wasn't that.

• • •

We numbly sped to the doctor's office, mute.

When we arrived, I urged him to leave me on the corner and go find parking. Blood was spilling down my legs as I stood there, on the bustling corner of West Third Street and Willaman Drive, across from the Cedars-Sinai towers. Waiting for the light to change, holding the unimaginable bag, shouting into the phone to my sister: "The baby FELL. OUT. She is IN A BAG." She couldn't believe that had possibly happened. I couldn't either. I still can't, all these years later.

With increasingly soaked towels still stuffed down my baggy sweatpants, I knew I wasn't going to stop bleeding until I delivered the placenta. In an effort to push the details of what was to come out of my mind, I recounted every detail of my miscarriage (thus far) to my sister while I shared a street with oblivious strangers.

"Wait, go back!" she said. "The baby came out while you were home alone?!"

"Yes," I replied. "She did. And I had to cut the umbilical cord. I have her in a bag right now so the doctor can do testing!" I wailed, the unfolding events unimaginable to me at sixteen weeks along. But what was even more unimaginable is that, on that busy street and as my life felt as though it was unraveling, people around me continued to live theirs. As I held the remains of my daughter in a bag, blood collecting in pools around my ankles, people were rushing past me to work or day care, a coffee date with a friend or a mundane errand. The contrast was nothing short of jarring.

As I started to disassociate from the duality of it all, I watched my life from a distance. And in the safety provided by that distance, I let the dread take hold. I felt suspended in midair, floating in the liminal space between life and death; a simultaneous place of trauma and disbelief, where the certainty that all life ends clashes with the sheer cruelty of an unexpected loss. I remember that, for a moment, I was terrified for my future self. *Now there's a dead baby. A hollow womb. What will come next? How will I mother, work, put one foot in front of the other, and grieve?* Amazing, the places our minds go.

I was bleeding incessantly, and I couldn't fathom how I'd take my pants off when I arrived at the doctor's office. But when she ushered me in, I heeded her orders to do so, and a blood clot the size of a boulder splattered across the floor. A nurse muttered that it looked like a "murder scene." She wasn't wrong—a death had occurred, and it had felt violent and cruel. The only way to make the bleeding stop was to extract the placenta, and that meant proceeding with a dilation and curettage (D&C), a procedure to remove it and any remaining tissue inside my uterus.

Before the procedure began, a nurse removed her from the plastic bag for testing, then placed her on the kind of tray you'd see surgical tools prepped on, where she stayed for the duration of my D&C. Her peaceful body was within eyeshot as mine continued to writhe.

I was faced with two options: wait for anesthesiology— numbing me for the painful mechanic extraction—and continue to bleed, then undergo a blood transfusion; or just get on with it unmedicated, pain, bloodlessness, and all. While I wanted desperately to not be in physical pain anymore, I was told that it could take the anesthesiologist up to an hour to arrive and administer the medication. If I chose to simply get it over with, the whole ordeal would be over in another ten or fifteen minutes, max. So, desperate for it all to end, I elected to press on without anesthesia. I couldn't imagine the fleeting pain would be any worse than the agony I already felt, emotionally and physically.

At some point, Jason entered the room. To this day I cannot recall from where or how, at what time or in what state. I can't tell you how he looked—was his face distraught with worry?—or if he asked my doctor for clarity on the next steps. I do, however, remember the rhythmic sound of his labored breath. He had been running. He ran to me. Now by my side, I asked Jason to turn some music on to help drown out the near-savage sound of the machine—to drown out the thoughts that accompanied those sounds.

Jason obliged and put on Alexi Murdoch's "All My Days," but the usually calming rhythm was woefully incapable of shielding me from the sounds that will always signify the final moments of my pregnancy. As the machine roared, I stared at the ceiling and felt everything I had prepared for—the sleepless nights breastfeeding my infant, the anxiety-ridden moments in which I would stare at my sleeping baby's chest rising and falling, the moment my son held his baby sister for the first time, the extra place setting at the dinner table—tugged from my body. As I clenched the nurse's hand and tears streamed down my face, I shifted my gaze to her—my stare piercing her soulful, almond-shaped eyes. And in her eyes I remained, until it was over. It took the full estimate—a brutal fifteen minutes—to ensure nothing had been left behind, save the part of me that still resides in that kind nurse's deep-brown eyes. The part of me desperate for a future I never had, a life I have never known. The part I knew I had to learn to live without.

At some point, my midwife friend, who had come over just the night before with her reassuring fetal doppler, also arrived. Like my husband, I cannot recall when or how. The only proof of her presence were the snapshots of the fetus she had the presence of mind to take. She just knew—an outcome of her education in birth and pregnancy loss, no doubt—that these pictures would prove useful in the future. That I would need them. That, eventually, I would want them.

After a few inhales of smelling salts and bites of salted crackers, and with nothing but those snapshots, my husband and I returned home. Assaulted by this new reality, I went blank.

• • •

The furthest thing from my mind following this incomprehensible trauma was to feel ashamed of it, as if I had done something wrong or like I should keep it secret. But I quickly found—both in my memory of so many of my patients' experiences, and prevalent in the research on women's feelings after pregnancy loss—that somehow shame is expected. It doesn't exactly make sense: One in four pregnancies ends in miscarriage—and that's just of the pregnancies that are known. (The number is probably much higher, due to chemical pregnancies, for example, where the expectant person may not have been aware a pregnancy even existed, much less that a miscarriage occurred.) Approximately one in one hundred pregnancies results in stillbirth. Others learn their developing babies are ill or won't make it to term, and therefore terminate for medical reasons. Still others must terminate based on health risk—in lieu of their own demise. One in eight couples struggles with conceiving a baby at all.

The medical facts are clear: A majority of miscarriages are due to chromosomal abnormalities, fetal complications, or other genetic issues. There are reportedly more than three million cases of miscarriage in the United States per year. This common occurrence is therefore a normative, albeit often difficult, outcome of pregnancy. But here's the thing: We are not in charge of chromosomes. And we ultimately have no control over genetics either.

Still, research has shown that *more than half* of people who have been through these ordeals feel guilty. More than a quarter feel shame.[1] And indeed, these concepts somehow have been ingrained in the psyches of countless people who've lost pregnancies—that their bodies were defective, that they failed, that they somehow did something bad, something wrong. Our culture literally adds insult to injury.

I couldn't tell you exactly why I didn't feel this way. I just didn't. Maybe it was because of my career, talking formerly pregnant people away from this very line of thinking, even though I had not yet experienced it firsthand. Maybe it was because I'd never believed miscarriage was the fault of any person. Regardless of the reasons why I was able to sidestep this self-destructive line of thought, I never once considered that I *did* something to prompt this traumatic loss.

But I also kept thinking, through the maze of grief and despair, how much worse it would be to also feel ashamed, guilty, or self-blaming. Amazing, the places our minds go. How much *more* agonizing it would be if I subscribed to the stigma, bought into society's expectations of women, and considered myself some kind of a defunct model solely because I couldn't carry this specific pregnancy to term. I shuddered to think how exponentially worse my suffering would be if I chose to stay silent.

I didn't want that for myself. And I didn't want it for anyone else either.

In time, I realized I wanted to make a dent in this taboo topic. I wanted to inspire women to question why they would turn this excruciating experience in on themselves. And I wanted to educate those who would blame women and other people capable of becoming pregnant for a reproductive outcome that was and is beyond their control. The best way I could think to reach the masses and provoke societal change was through words. Starting with my own.

I wasn't ready to share my story immediately after my loss. I had told countless patients prior to my own pregnancy loss experience that grief doesn't adhere to a timeline, and that healing from any traumatic experience is a cyclical event with no beginning or definitive end. So in the days, weeks, and months that followed, I tried to practice what I preached. Sometimes I felt like I was ready, only to sit in front of a computer and become excruciatingly aware that I was not. Other times, I simply knew it was too soon, and in those moments I had to remind myself that sharing my loss with anyone should be a choice, not a requirement. I wanted to eventually divulge this information publicly, yes, but on my own terms and when it felt "right" for me and me alone.

Eventually, in early October 2014, two years after my loss, I plopped down at my desk and began writing what turned out to be a searing piece detailing what I'd lived through. Once completed, I sent it into the largest, most influential outlet I could think of, with the hope of not only sharing my experience but sparking a much-needed reproductive revolution of sorts. As soon as the *New York Times* accepted my essay to run on Pregnancy and Infant Loss Awareness Day, October 15, I reached out to a talented calligrapher to see if she would be willing to make some signs I could hold for a photo that would accompany the essay. The sign would read "#IHadaMiscarriage" but I would be faceless in it, so that anyone and everyone could picture themselves holding the very same sign. I wanted to send an unabashed message into the world, and this seemed like the best way I could think of to get conversations rolling about this all-too-common, albeit all-too-neglected, topic. The hashtag hearkened back to my frenzied early text messages to my friends and family, when I'd searched for a feeling of community and the grounding presence, even if it was via the phone, of those who would support me. I wanted to create a national discussion that, in some way, would do the same for those who had experienced the same type of loss. #IHadaMiscarriage would be more than a transference of information. It was meant as a call to action. It was meant as an invitation. It was meant to incite an influx of silenced stories. It was meant to normalize grief and invite those who have felt shamed into silence to share theirs as they find comfort and solidarity in others.

And almost two years to the day after my miscarriage, my piece ran, with the image boldly alongside it. I logged on to my Twitter account and watched as people around the world chimed in with their reproductive hopes and hardships, and shared feelings they no longer wanted to keep silent. It was clear: women worldwide were yearning for a cultural shift, one that would allow these stories to flow freely rather than remain shrouded. A simultaneous sense of relief and overwhelm washed over me as I received emails from people who had survived pregnancy and infant loss and continued putting one foot in front of the other in the aftermath.

I vowed that this was just the beginning. I kept writing. It was as if I couldn't get myself to stop. I put pen to paper and dove into various aspects of pregnancy loss and life after, as it was clear this was not only helping me process my feelings, but also inspiring others to do the same.

To spread the message further, I started an Instagram account: @IHadaMiscarriage. The followers came in by the thousands. It was clear there was not only a willingness, but a burning desire and a pressing need to shift the cultural landscape by opening a dialogue for all who have experienced these painful losses. And as the number of followers continued to increase, it also became apparent that a primal need to be in communion with others, in both grief and hope, was driving the collective demand for the silence surrounding miscarriage and infant loss to end. Women no longer wanted to do this alone. These women wanted their voices to be heard. These women wanted to step out of the shadows.

My Instagram page became a hub where people could share their loss stories, find fellowship, and receive support. The page grew into a place for people to talk candidly about grief and their complex feelings of failure, fear, indifference, relief, desperation, and isolation. A place to share openly about their seedlings of hope, their crushing disappointment, the messiness of moving "forward," and, in some cases, the freedom of letting their reproductive dreams go entirely. They would meet in the comments and become real-life friends. They'd support one another through both subsequent losses and successful pregnancies. They'd share parenting hacks, relationship advice, lament about quirky in-laws, and discuss the inconsequential moments of their lives that, in the midst of a loss, can feel overwhelming. For many, they found an online home.

What emerged from a simple hashtag and a personal essay was far from what I had initially planned, but the #IHadaMiscarriage campaign took on a life of its own. What began as a social media endeavor quickly evolved into a robust multiplatform effort. It was even the subject of an academic study exploring the shared experience of miscarriage and how it's discussed online.[2] To this day, on an annual basis, I use the movement to highlight various aspects of pregnancy and infant loss worthy of further investigation.

As my voice in this space grew, national media outlets

reached out to me to speak on the topic. I inadvertently became one of the go-to psychologists in the media on the topic of pregnancy and infant loss. It was clear: the world seemed more poised than ever to shine light on a dark subject.

Today, I have an eager and robust community on Instagram joining me in rethinking why there's trepidation and stigma around saying, "I had a miscarriage." There isn't a day that goes by that I don't receive a message or see a comment along the lines of "I refuse to silence my pain any longer. This community has helped me see that I am not alone," and I am further reminded of the power of replacing the silence, stigma, and shame with the truth of our experiences. I've collected more stories than I ever thought possible, communicating with people across the world as they navigate their own reproductive roller coasters. People tell me that the @IHadaMiscarriage Instagram account is one of the first places they turned to after experiencing a pregnancy loss, especially since the relative anonymity of the social media world can shield people from the stigma of miscarriage that is far too often perpetuated by even the most well-intended family members, friends, partners, and loved ones.

My role borne out of the #IHadaMiscarrige movement is one I take seriously, and I'm forever honored to be even a small part of people's journeys toward sharing their experiences. In turn, some of the community members have graciously allowed me to share the words they've given me—in direct-message conversations, in comments, in email threads—here in this very book. They, along with the women I see in my practice, have taught me so much about the extensive power of words and the necessity of vulnerability. Sharing inspires me—and, I hope, others—to dig deeper into aspects of grief and loss and life after.

Galvanizing a community in this way has been transformative beyond measure, but still—I am not without grief. I'm not sure I *believe* in grief disappearing altogether as a possibility. I don't see healing as finite. I'm still in my grief on occasion, and that's okay. My loss ultimately gave birth to a movement. And now I've got to raise it up.

## 2

*"I failed to give myself the space to fall apart."*

Early in my training en route to becoming a psychologist, I learned that a common reaction to traumatic events is a kind of "perseverance approach." Referred to in the Diagnostic and Statistical Manual (the go-to guide for mental health) as the "acute stress response," this is a prime example of the "fight" part of the fight-flight-or-freeze response, which can accompany perceived danger or harmful situations. This physiological reaction to stress is an adaptive mechanism employed with the hopes of shirking danger. *I. Must. Survive.* In day-to-day life, this response can take many forms. Sometimes people try on an "I can handle this, I'm okay" attitude in order to push ahead. This is a sincere (and often unconscious) attempt at "moving forward" so as not to sink into the wretched, lonely pit of mourning that so often accompanies trauma. With the loss of a would-be pregnancy, this acute stress response can manifest as anxiety, difficulty concentrating, a sense of impending doom, and/or denial, among other things. We so desperately want to hold on to the life we knew before, untouched by this particular heartache. And so we claw at the walls of our past—comforting walls we knew so well once upon a time. But for so many of us, unavoidably, the profundity of this remarkable experience eventually sets in. And how could it not? We can only stave off pain so long before it comes careening in and shoves its way smack-dab front and center. Trauma has that way about it.

Ready or not, here it comes.

• • •

Even as a psychologist, despite knowing what I know from all my years of completing doctoral hoops, barreling through piles of trauma-related textbooks, and talking with other individuals in the midst of their own traumas' far-reaching reverberations, my post-loss journey was filled with a complicated mix of haphazard attempts at honing that innate survival instinct. Beleaguered and besieged by losing the pregnancy, I focused on putting one foot in front of the other. Day by day. I did my best to continue on. I showed up. I stayed busy. I chimed in. I replied. And on occasion, I smiled, even.

I thought I was okay, but I wasn't.

Still, I kept moving.

• • •

"I'm concerned, Jess. I really feel like you should give yourself more time," my sister said lovingly but determinedly upon hearing that I was planning to return to work just four days after my miscarriage. Her concern was clear as we spoke on the phone that evening. She knew what I couldn't seem to surmise on my own: it wasn't yet time. Of course, it wasn't. But I was not convinced.

"I feel like I can handle it," I pushed back gently, in the hopes I might sway her. "Also, I can't just leave my patients in a lurch. I don't want them to worry about *me*, after all. Sitting around isn't helping ease this pain either."

If I sat in silence for too long, I could still hear the sound of my own piercing scream as it reverberated off the glass walls of our house. I needed a raison d'être, a purpose, or basically anything that would pull me out of my own poignancy. And I needed it badly.

"It'll have only been four days." She repeated herself. "*Four days!* Your loss happened Thursday; you can't just return to your office on Monday. You can't. It makes no sense. Your patients will understand, and it's best for you *and* for them that you take a few more days to recover."

She was right. I knew she was. I just hadn't given myself the space to really think through not only my options but the potential ramifications of whatever I decided. It was clear that I wasn't considering my *own* needs, my recovery, my drained body and mind. And I appreciated her compassionate attention to this very important detail of my life postmiscarriage. What a loving act this was, to care for me when I clearly wasn't able to do so for myself. So while I dreaded sitting in my grief, and navigating whatever that would inevitably look like, I was forced, through my sister's grace, to slow down.

"I hear you," I replied, both scared and relieved that my sister stuck to her guns and saw the light when I couldn't. "I'll email my patients now and explain that I'll return to the office next Monday instead of this coming Monday. And thank you, sis. Thank you for guiding me here."

Agreeing to slow down did not mean I would stop moving entirely though, and my sister's concern could not convince me that I didn't have to remain in a perpetual state of motion. Spending time alone in my head replaying the dreaded details of that day seemed untenable, cruel, even. If I kept moving, maybe the trauma wouldn't catch up to me and swallow me whole.

I didn't see it then, and it took me a number of years to properly identify that I had failed to give myself what I needed most in the moments following my pregnancy loss: the space to fall apart. Despite my professional poise, this painstaking grief was unraveling me, slowly but surely, and no amount of driving power to push forward could keep me from eventually crumbling.

Looking back, I realize my attempts to press on were an effort to reinhabit my pre-loss life, as it were. I wanted order, predictability, and peace—the antithesis of the psychological chaos my miscarriage yielded. And in my mind, I could find it all again safely inside my office. Getting back to my patients and those meaningful sessions with them felt like exactly the balm and the rich interaction I'd been craving. I wanted to dive back in—to sit with my patients, and to foster some semblance of regularity. On some level, I probably knew that in the grander scheme, taking only a week and a few days to recover from the physical and emotional trauma of what had occurred was nowhere near enough time, but I needed to reengage—to dive back into my purpose-driven work. *This is an act of self-preservation*, I told myself. *This is the work of rebuilding.*

But when I returned to work, it became increasingly clear just how affected I was and how ineffectual my attempts at outrunning my grief had been. Before I returned to sitting in my therapy chair, it didn't seem concerning to me that my work was inextricably linked to this type of trauma, that the kinds of exercises I had to put my mind through in my office would offer no escape from what was already echoing inside it. Only the week before, I had been able to sit and listen, as my job called for, without having any thoughts about myself. But in a race to sidestep the emotional aftermath of my pregnancy loss, I had sprinted toward a space where loss, grief, trauma, mourning, and the complex ways in which we process it all were discussed at length. I could no longer keep thoughts of my own life siloed from what my patients discussed with me. I had been exposed to the anguish and experiences of my patients' journeys through very similar traumas. Once again, there was no going back.

. . .

I will not soon forget the first session I had upon my return to work; sitting across from Kate,* a thirtysomething patient I'd been seeing for several years. It just so happened that our meeting coincided with her first trip back to my office in months; our sessions had been on intermission, as she'd recently given birth to her third child.

We sat together in my office, aglow in the fall light, and remarked to each other how nice it was to be together again. As the session began, I felt present, measured. Sitting across from her felt familiar and warm, and I was thankful to be back in my seat and once again facilitate vulnerable moments with people brave enough to reveal buried aspects

*Names and details of patients, community members, and friends have been altered to protect confidentiality and maintain anonymity.

of themselves. I also welcomed the opportunity to continue concentrating on something other than my own grief. I was focused on Kate, and wholly glad to be.

"How have you been?" I asked.

"Um . . ." Her voice wavered as she stammered through her answer. Judging by her body language, I could tell that she was struggling. "I've been okay, I guess. Well, sort of." She trailed off, then changed her answer: "Sometimes, actually . . . no, I haven't. I don't know." Tears welled up in her eyes and started falling down her rosy cheeks. "I'm sorry . . ." she whispered. "I didn't want to start crying so quickly. My hormones are all over the place, and I just don't feel like myself these days. I feel pretty low, confused, even."

"I'm so sorry to hear this," I said reassuringly. "This is such a tender time. Such a big transition. *Another* big, life-changing transition."

As soon as those words escaped my lips, I heard them—I mean *actually* heard them. They knocked the wind out of me. Or rather, I knocked the wind out of myself.

As Kate wept and spoke about those complicated feelings that can inevitably accompany the fourth trimester after a newborn enters the world, I worked to remain present and calm. Beneath the surface, though, I noticed the pace of my breath shift ever so slightly. I also noticed a warmth overtake my weary body. Not a comforting warmth though, more like a here-come-the-cold-sweats-post-body-heat-up from *my* postpartum hormones, but with no baby to show for them. Feelings resembling—though not quite manifesting as—an anxiety attack. Because there, across from me, sat a woman in exactly the position I'd thought I was working toward: deep in postpartum adjustments, new baby, full breasts, hair pulled up as an afterthought into a messy top knot. Her hands were full in a psychological sense, and her arms were full in a literal one. Three children.

Her. But not me.

Somehow, I made it to the end of my workday, although I couldn't say how I managed given the complexities that surfaced in my mind, time and time again. And when I finally climbed into my car and closed the door, all I had been running from finally caught up to me. It took over my body, seared my insides, and then poured out of me with reckless abandon. I tossed my purse onto the passenger seat, slumped forward, and held my bereft face in my hands. I cried great, heaving sobs until I exhausted myself of all emotion. My tears fell from my eyes like rain. I longed to go back in time, to undo this grand loss, to return to the before-loss me. Now, there was only post-loss me to familiarize myself with, and I didn't want to know her at all. I knew it wasn't possible to go back and live whatever life I was headed toward, before the blood and the bathroom. But I also knew there was so much I didn't know about what was to come, what I'd have to soldier through in the months to follow, or how this unknown would change me in ways both big and small. Loss divided time into "before" and "after," and I felt suspended between them both.

With nowhere to go—no way to move forward or backward—I sank into an unnerving sense of vulnerability. *Why me?* I thought. *Why me? But then again*, I challenged myself, *why* not *me?* I knew the statistics of pregnancy loss, just as I knew the complexities of grief and reproductive trauma. I had studied them in depth. I had incorporated them into my daily life. I had dedicated my career to them. How could I have allowed myself to be so surprised by an outcome I had spent countless hours assisting others in traversing?

At some point along the way, I must have compartmentalized my professional life and my personal life, putting them neatly in two distinct places in my head. The result, it seemed, was that it never quite dawned on me how swiftly and deftly they could become tangled up with each other. This was a level of vulnerability and raw exposure that I'd never imagined. My heart had been pried open, and I was swelling with emotion so profoundly it hurt.

Retrospect can be such an astute teacher. I've learned this the hard way (as if there's any other way to learn this). In the initial days and weeks that followed my miscarriage, I think it was primarily adrenaline that powered me through. *Must survive. Must continue. Must do.* But then, when I finally grasped just how eviscerated I really was, I couldn't dodge the eventual downfall. This was only the beginning.

...

A couple of weeks after my miscarriage, I ventured out to my usual place in Hollywood to get a pedicure. I had been confined to my office and my home, and I was just trying to do something that felt familiar. Prosaic. *Normal.* I wasn't necessarily looking forward to it, but it seemed like a smart step to take. Self-care, I figured, was a good thing to add to the to-do list, especially at a time like this. I thought I'd do something mindless and comforting and be okay. After all, it was just a twelve-minute drive from home down the winding hill of Laurel Canyon to Sunset Boulevard. When I arrived at the upbeat nail salon, predominantly filled with older women, I was greeted by Joanna, a heavyset Romanian woman who has been painting my toes since before my pregnancy with Liev. We had shared much with one another during those years, and whether we were swapping prideful parenting milestones or commiserating in frustration about Los Angeles traffic, I was always happy to see her. "What's the matter?" she queried lovingly. "You look sad." Apprehensively, I shared my news. Tears reflexively began to roll down my freckled cheeks as I spit out truncated pieces of the atrocious experience I barely survived. I didn't want to overwhelm her with all the gory details, or gross her out by telling her about the stream of blood or the baby in a plastic bag or the sickening feeling, housed permanently in my bones, of the placenta being yanked out during the unmedicated D&C procedure. But I felt comforted by her and comfortable sharing the gist of my story with her. We held eye contact as her tears welled up in astonishment. An empathic droplet fell from her squinty blue eye as we held hands in solidarity. She'd lost a pregnancy, too, she explained. Decades prior to my own. I hadn't known about her miscarriage until I shared mine, but why would I have? We're conditioned to not share these stories. We've become accustomed to living parallel to one another, oblivious of the pain we're all trying to overcome.

As we held on to each other, I couldn't help but worry that I had inadvertently wounded her in some way with my proverbial reproductive war story. Or perhaps triggered her own tough memories unexpectedly. But I couldn't hold on to this thought long. It vanished as quickly as it had seared my mind's eye. In a split second, I lost my steadiness. I felt awash in confusion, suddenly unsure of how I had even gotten there. Another one of trauma's unforeseeable effects: briefly succumbing to overwhelmingly intense emotions, promptly followed by full-body exhaustion and a disengagement so severe you can practically disassociate. Taken over by bodily sensitivity and what feels like an emotional storm, you realize that trauma is a depleting game of mind-body pinball.

I called my husband from the spa chair, disoriented. I was buzzing with an uncanny sense of fear. *What is going on?* This became my unwanted mantra. Almost all I could think, on repeat: *What is going on?* "Please come! Jay, I need you to sit here with me," I pleaded. "I don't know how I got here. I'm not sure if I can get myself home." By the time he arrived, I was trembling with head-to-toe chills, despite having my feet submerged in the warm, soapy water Joanna had prepared for me. As the anxiety continued to carve ruthless paths inside my body, I felt miles away from the water, the chair, Joanna, and myself.

Jason's mere presence shifted my energy almost immediately, but I needed his words too. Words of reassurance, and maybe even a wild guess as to why I was feeling so disoriented and foreign in my own body. Not that he would actually be able to pinpoint the reason why—how could he?—but his sheer attempt at wondering aloud with me about the *why now?* brought me calm. This exchange—of words and tenderness—eventually ushered me back to the present. To the chair. To the water. To Joanna. To my life.

• • •

Disassociation became my norm. I was an active participant and a bystander in my life, at various moments, and without so much as a warning.

Places that I used to go without a second thought became triggers—I couldn't stand to be in the supermarket, or the dry cleaner's. Doing the regular day-to-day things we all do suddenly heightened my anxiety, and my eventual awareness of it, alerting me to just how altered I was—how off I actually felt. Mundane errands I'd done my entire adult life became disquieting. This unstructured time—when I wasn't at work or with my family—allowed newfound anxiousness room to pierce, prod, and flirt without abandon. Time off—what most consider to be freedom, what my well-intentioned sister assumed would be beneficial—just created unlimited space for disquietude. These moments offered blank spaces for my mind, which slowly filled to the brim with excessive uneasiness. I felt incapable of deviating from my routine at all in those initial weeks. It was so vulnerable—so exposed—to be outside the plan.

I began to avoid errands altogether, but not every area of my life could be put on hold. I had to pull over to fill my tank with gas on occasion, for example, but these instances of necessity were not without a fair bit of bargaining. *Maybe I can wait to fill up the car until tomorrow*, I thought more than once. *Maybe I can make it home and back to work again before the red light comes on. One more day without an errand, please! Just one more day.* Jason and I had pretty much always shared the load of household chores, but in the aftermath of my loss he took over the stuff outside of the house: food shopping, dry cleaning, pharmacy runs, child pickup and drop-off. My cortisol levels needed a respite, it seemed. Home and work were all I could manage.

• • •

Therapy was a natural place for me to turn. I had been seeing my own therapist, Valerie, for just over a decade, and she'd seen me through so much in the time we'd known each other—graduate studies, career pursuits, relationships, my marriage to Jason, and Liev's birth—so turning to her now was instinctual. The day after my miscarriage, I left Valerie a message. I called her reflexively, without thinking, almost the way one would call their mother after a seismic life event: "Valerie, it's Jessica Zucker. Please call me back as soon as possible. I had a miscarriage. The baby fell out while I was home alone. I'd like to schedule a time to connect as soon as you can. Thank you."

Click.

Numb.

Valerie is the one who absorbed all the pieces.

...

I had known Valerie since moving to Boston in my late twenties, when I was working at the Harvard School of Public Health, and during my studies of psychology and gender there as well. Back then, I wasn't necessarily going through anything that had a pressing need for treatment per se, but I'd pretty much always welcomed therapy as a tremendously helpful and unlocking mainstay, and embraced the opportunity to benefit from it. So I had asked a relatively new friend, Aliza, whom I'd met at a yoga studio up the road from my third-floor walk-up in Cambridge, to ask her therapist for referrals. Aliza was smart, and I trusted that her therapist would know some quality professionals in the area. She did: she knew Valerie.

Valerie's office was walking distance from my old apartment, crouched over the rhododendron trees just steps from Harvard Yard. I still remember that first session: I arrived early, clutching a small cup of coffee to warm my hands. I was not yet used to the bite of Boston's fall weather and how it differed from what I had grown accustomed to in Manhattan. Still a newbie, I was prone to holding warm things whenever I ventured out, hoping to make the nip less intimidating. Even though therapy was far from unfamiliar to me, I caught myself feeling apprehensive about this first meeting. As I flipped through the magazines in her waiting room, I couldn't help but wonder how much I'd share in that initial fifty-minute session—where would I even begin? There's an inevitable awkwardness to the retelling of your life story.

But that session was deeply helpful, as were countless others that followed on a weekly basis. I credit therapy with providing the framework and the ultimate haven of safety—the place where I could lay it all out and sift through everything, piece by piece. Valerie became a source of unparalleled insight and a maternal beacon of sorts who has helped soften—dare I say relinquish—some of my festering childhood wounds. The word "gratitude" pales in comparison to how I feel about her and her important role in my life. Even though I moved from Boston to Los Angeles a handful of years after we first met in the confines of her cozy, book-lined office, where I would sit on her firm, hunter-green velvet couch in search of comfort, she seemed to understand me in a way I wouldn't be able to replicate, so when I relocated, I continued seeing her over Skype and through phone calls. She was particularly helpful during my own studies to become a therapist myself a few years later. A therapist really needs a good therapist.

...

A few days after my miscarriage, that familiar face of hers crinkled in shock on my laptop screen as I spewed the horror of that fateful day: October 11, 2012. Valerie was there; to hold my story, the utter disbelief, that pulverized heart of mine, my unyielding astonishment, grief's hangover. She was there through it all, a witness to the multifarious layers: the anger outbursts, the moments I clung to denial, and was there when I flirted with hope in fits and starts. She was there just as she had always been.

My seemingly disturbing, far-flung feelings (which I soon learned are the norm) were met with understanding, and it was here I could roll around in the grief, roar about resentments, shriek in horror of the events I'd navigated. Here I had permission to get messy in the heinous struggle I so badly wished wasn't mine.

Over the course of our sessions, Valerie and I explored what it was like to live in a worn-down body and a fractured psyche after enduring this specific kind of trauma. Although she opts not to speak in clinical language or diagnostic terminology with her patients—and therefore, I wasn't formally diagnosed with post-traumatic stress disorder—together, we began to see how this trauma changed various aspects of my life. The symptoms of my trauma accompanied me through my days (and nights) for too long to remember. This is, of course, not unique to my experience—research has found that approximately four in ten women experience symptoms of PTSD after miscarriage.[3] And several of PTSD's hallmark signs—intrusive memories, irritability, emotional detachment, severe anxiety, to name a few—became the territory I now navigated. But memorizing statistics and perusing scientific studies to better treat my patients turned out to be far different than coming face-to-face with an awareness of the precariousness of mortality firsthand. The me that existed before my loss could compartmentalize the science from the personal and separate lived experiences from the hard data in order to provide those in need with perspective and guidance. But the me that existed after could not. Now, I was a statistic. Now, I was stuck replaying the visuals and the physical feelings associated with death occurring in my body.

Valerie was there when I realized that I had thought I was okay, but I wasn't. And because of the hour we spent together each week, I eventually puttered out and ultimately stopped moving. Through the consistency of her emotional presence and our extensive conversations, at long last, I allowed myself to stand still and fall apart.

· · ·

On the other six days of the week—the days I didn't speak with Valerie—putting pen to paper and leaking the trauma onto the page was a godsend. Typing away on my keyboard became synonymous with a semblance of salvation. It was there, on those pages—the published ones, the eventual Instagram captions, even the ones hidden away in a Microsoft Word file that never saw the light of day—that I connected with myself profoundly, in a sort of meditation on pain. Writing had been something I loved, always—be it journaling, working on papers during both of my master's degree programs, undertaking my award-winning dissertation, or crafting published pieces—but during this time, writing became a true conduit for survival. The empty pages don't judge; in fact, they are begging for emotions to be unleashed upon them. Blank pages were there to receive my

stories, and by telling and retelling over and over again —
whether the words were hesitant or free-flowing, whether
they were simplistic or robust—I created pathways to
lean toward my rawest self, no matter how distressing and
befuddling the feelings I found there were. But soon my
need to create in the name of self-preservation morphed
into something new, something capable of encompassing
far more than my traumatic loss. As I continued to write,
I started to hope that my words would do for others what
they were able to do for me: dig trenches and form pathways through loss, grief, trauma, and mourning, so that
those who felt their own variation of the same trauma I had
been enduring could also find a way to stop running from
the person that miscarriage, pregnancy, and infant loss had
made them to be. I started to envision a scenario in which
the pages honoring my own loss would assist someone in
finding a unique and personal way to honor their own.

By writing my way into the depths of my heartache
and engaging in conversations with Valerie that acted as a
life preserver, pulling me back to the surface, I was able to
inch closer to a calling I had not yet yielded: a call to action
that would unveil the crushing pain I was consciously and
unconsciously attempting to ward off, and, in doing so, give
silent permission for others to unabashedly do the same.

3

*"The strident trifecta: silence, stigma, and shame."*

Pregnancy and infant loss have been a constant since the dawn of time. And not just for humans. It's been discovered that humans and nonhumans alike experience grief after the loss of a pregnancy or infant. One animal study found that chimpanzee mothers whose infants died carried around the mummified remains of their babies for up to two months.[4] Similar behavior has been observed in elephants, giraffes, and marine mammals.[5] In addition to observing marked behavioral changes in animal life upon losing offspring—such as listlessness, standing vigil, the refusal of food and companionship—researchers have pinpointed animal grief through hormonal changes in females who have lost a baby, namely an increase in stress hormones called glucocorticoids.[6] Suffice it to say, this kind of primal reaction to sudden death is not a human construct. We do not have a monopoly on grief. It is the cultural associations and reactions around it that we are responsible for, and those have changed significantly over time.

As far back as ancient legends, the theme of losing a

pregnancy or infant as a consequence for bad behavior, perceived failure, or generational transgressions is fairly prevalent. In many cultures, miscarriage and stillbirth are conceptualized, even now, as direct punishment for wrong-doing; affiliation with sorcery, supernatural elements, or evil spirits; or the breach of a taboo by the pregnant woman. I have extensively researched other cultures' perceptions of miscarriage, wanting to explore those beyond my own as a Jewish American woman to get a sense of global patterns (or lack thereof). For example, the conceptualization of pregnancy and infant loss as being a direct consequence of negative actions has been seen in Malawi, among the Maasai community, and in western Kenya, where it is believed that a woman's wrongdoing might result in pregnancy loss.[7]

Certain countries have a unique perspective on preg-nancy and infant loss due to the prevalence of their infant survival rates. Faced with the high probability of losing their babies, these women fortify their emotions until they know the baby will last. In Nigeria, for example, where infant and child mortality rates are high, mourning is not a practice incorporated into culture. In fact, given the rates of loss, newborns aren't recognized as true members of soci-ety until they've surpassed infancy. And in Brazil, where infant survival rates are low, researchers have observed that maternal attachment and bonding are a far more grad-ual process than the one we observe in the United States. In Bijnor District, located in northern India, pregnancy itself is considered a "matter of shame," and is there-fore not widely discussed or celebrated. Being proud of pregnancy is frowned upon. The loss of a pregnancy is ren-dered a nonevent, with no rituals or communal support to accompany it.[8]

...

For as long as I've been researching, thinking, and writing about miscarriage, I've been aware of a strident trifecta that accompanies the topic: silence, stigma, and shame. These three concepts are responsible for so many of the challenges we face when it comes to pregnancy and infant loss. They work in concert at nearly all times, obstructing conversations and connection around this all-too-common topic, and isolating those who experience it. While they're inextricably linked, they are part of a vicious cycle that actually has a starting point. And culturally speaking, a relatively easy one to trace.

In the Western world, there have been periods where we actually weren't nearly as hesitant to talk about the experience as we are today. For one thing, at a time when methods of birth control were virtually nonexistent, and abortion was illegal and therefore dangerous, some women welcomed miscarriage as a relief—financially, physically—from carrying and caring for more children.[9] There was no reason not to put voice to that feeling. It was described in articles in the 1800s as a blessing, nature doing its job. But miscarriage and pregnancy loss could also be very dangerous for women; infection and even death were possible outcomes. It was imperative to *not* stay completely silent, lest you jeopardize your own life.[10]

There have been glimpses of this more vocal approach in recent decades, like in the 1970s, when the modern wellness trend was really born, and miscarriage became a public health issue. Women began demanding answers when they noticed pregnancy losses corresponding with safety issues like pesticide use and hazardous living conditions. We were shouting, begging to be noticed and taken seriously.[11] But by and large, silence has been the norm. Especially as the twentieth century drew to a close, and access to safe, legal abortion care became constitutional law due to the passage of *Roe v. Wade* and birth control became more attainable than it had ever been before, things started changing. The prevailing narrative, especially among white, middle- and upper-class women, became that, essentially, all "kept" pregnancies are *wanted* pregnancies.

Advances in modern medicine have also been both a help and a hindrance. We can now know we are pregnant sooner than ever: tests can catch a pregnancy days before a missed period, and at just six weeks, before women may even know they're pregnant, fetal heart tones—more commonly known as the "heartbeat"—can be detected. Advances in sonography and the introduction of 3-D ultrasounds magnify fetuses so they appear as large, and as fully formed, as infants. And so, the gestational lengths of our pregnancies rarely dictate our emotional response to them—for so many of us, they seem *real* the moment they begin and the connection only strengthens from there. And while the medical gains of these scientific feats cannot be understated, they have both expanded and complicated our collective reaction to pregnancy loss. Instead of being a blessing or a medical necessity, a public-health concern or a consequence of a past misdeed, miscarriage is now often associated with just one word: "grief." And for the generations that came before us, grief was often considered a private emotion. Our mothers and grandmothers didn't grow up in a culture where openness and dialogue about pregnancy and infant loss was encouraged, and they did not have the language to pass along to us. We have been kept underground.[12]

Silence has even become encoded in medical recommendations. It's common practice in the medical community to suggest women wait to share their pregnancy news until they are "out of the woods." In obstetric terms, that generally means waiting until after the first trimester, or around twelve weeks, when the likelihood of miscarriage is statistically lower and screenings that help determine the chance of a fetal abnormality have been conducted. Once the first trimester passes, the conventional wisdom goes, you've reached an ostensible safe zone—a time to celebrate and let your baby bump show. When you begin to unpack the messaging of "wait until the second trimester," the logic goes something like this: "Don't share your good news until you are in the clear. This way, if your good news becomes bad news, then you won't have to share your bad news."

Stop and think about this—really think. By suggesting that women stay mum during these preliminary weeks and in the event of an early miscarriage, we essentially remove from the conversation—and in so doing, stigmatize—any woman who doesn't experience multiple trimesters of pregnancy. It implies that you probably won't want to or shouldn't share news of a miscarriage, so you shouldn't say anything until the risk of that happening is lower.

To be clear, it's completely understandable if you'd like to keep news of your pregnancy to yourself for however long, and for whatever reason. Miscarriages are undoubtedly hard and, for some women, they can be difficult to discuss. But it's worth reflecting on whether you're consciously choosing not to share the details of your personal medical history or reflexively avoiding these conversations because it's so ingrained in us not to talk about loss. Not to talk about grief. Or worse, if you are going underground with your feelings based on self-blame or guilt.

The reality is, a miscarriage at any stage might require support, and when we encourage women to be hush-hush in the early weeks of pregnancy, we're potentially robbing them of that support should they need it. Opening up about loss and expressing grief (candidly and unabashedly—or any reaction, for that matter) can create a sense of community and connectedness during an otherwise isolating time. It also might inspire others to do the same. Grief, like all emotions, affects everyone differently, and sometimes we don't have a clue what we need in the throes of our despair until we are forced to survive it. We cannot assume the stage of gestation will automatically determine the potential impact of a pregnancy loss—it does not. The pain of sharing or not sharing a loss that evokes feelings of grief, mourning, longing, or self-hate, whether it happens at five weeks or forty, is poignant and individual.

I was raised as a culturally Jewish woman and taught to believe that life begins at birth—that birth is the moment when a fetus is deemed a person. Because of that teaching, I found some comfort in the idea that I didn't lose a life, but the promise of one. And as such, I didn't initially relate to women who, for example, upon seeing a positive pregnancy test, immediately felt spiritually connected to the idea of who this future baby might be. Over time and after exposure to various perspectives and women's stories, I've come to appreciate the myriad ways people feel about pregnancy and their connection to it. No matter how we interpret what is growing in our bodies, pregnancy, and/or its personhood, we have the right to grieve upon losing it and the boundless possibilities of a future that did not come to fruition. We also have the right to feel relieved, or even indifferent, about a loss without feeling judged. We have the right to mourn the milestones reached only in the most hopeful recesses of our minds—the first steps that were never walked, the first words that were never spoken. And we deserve to do so without assigning blame to ourselves or downplaying our emotional reactions, whatever they may be, as the result of society's inability to sit uncomfortably in grief, or any other response to miscarriage discussed in hushed, whispered tones. We need to remind one another of this very fact—the fact that there is no one at fault here, and no one is defined by the ways in which they navigate the aftermath—by refusing to sit in silence.

Because regardless of what we feel as individual women, the end result of encouraging silence on a societal level is stigma and, quite possibly, shame. We gravitate away from what we do not understand; we cannot understand what we don't discuss. And it takes an incredible amount of courage to break away from an accepted norm, making dialogues all the rarer. Because of our culture of secrecy, many of us believe that miscarriage is uncommon; one survey found more than half of respondents believed that fewer than 5 percent of pregnancies end in miscarriage.[13] And that survey shows just how widespread other related misinformation is: most respondents believed women could cause miscarriages by their actions, including experiencing stress or lifting something heavy, and nearly a quarter of respondents thought that the use of contraception, alcohol, or tobacco could result in miscarriage.[14] These answers are so, so far from the truth, which is that most miscarriages are the result of chromosomal abnormalities.[15] And this is where we're starting from—a place of cultural misunderstanding amplified and perpetuated by solitude and shame. This is what we have to work with: a culture that thinks miscarriage is *our* fault. How can we fix it unless we talk about it?

Combine silence and stigma and you'll inevitably reach the most personalized and arguably the most complicated spoke in the trifecta: shame. It's a natural endpoint, the unfair result of having to internalize our thoughts when we can't put a voice to them, and the fear that even if we did speak them, we'd be judged. Judged for doing something "wrong." Or maybe we believe we *did* do something wrong. One of the reasons the grief from miscarriage is so complex is that our own bodies, which we believe we can control in so many aspects, are the very site of the loss. It is all happening within us, both literally and figuratively. This can make it understandably hard to translate the pain in a way others can understand. But that truth also increases the likelihood that we hold ourselves responsible. And shame is an incredibly difficult feeling to sit with. It devours from within, feeding on the guilt and self-blame it fosters in a never-ending cycle. It festers and overtakes our sense of self. Shame is perhaps best known for its propensity to spiral. I hear these thoughts all the time, both in the confines of my practice and in conversation with other women: "How could I let this happen?" "My body failed. It doesn't work. I'm broken." "If only I had/hadn't exercised." "I'm defective." "I'm scared to tell anyone I was ambivalent about motherhood—they'll think that's why I lost the pregnancy."

• • •

Celeste's gaze was averted as she lay on my couch ascribing blame to herself for her recent loss. "I am bad. This happened to me because of *me*. Something is deeply wrong with me. Everyone but me can get pregnant and stay pregnant," she said as she stared at the ceiling, cheeks hot pink, blushing with strong feelings.

Celeste's early life may have set the stage for this way of thinking. Her mother, she recalled, had been depressed and overwhelmed ever since Celeste could remember. When Celeste was in utero, her mother—pregnant with twins—was put on bed rest in the middle of her second trimester. During labor, one of the babies died. Celeste was born healthy and thriving, but her would-be sibling did not make it. Mourning through the transition to motherhood, her mother found it tough to fully engage, to be fully present with her living child, which presumably affected the basic mirroring babies require. Bonding and attachment were compromised. Without these elemental building blocks, the development of self-esteem can be stymied. If not remedied, lack of maternal attunement can show itself as a shaky self-concept later in life, paving the way for habitual self-blame. For Celeste, this meant rampant shame burrowing its way into what she perceived to be personal failures. So, when she learned she'd had an ectopic pregnancy, she assumed it was her fault.

"You believe this happened because of something inside of you, because of who you are," I said.

"Yes," she replied, "I am flawed."

Celeste's expressed feelings of shame epitomize the self-blaming cycle. She loses track of herself in mazes of guilt and flagrant self-hate as she attempts to make her way in the world. Adulthood has proven tough. Shame rears its vicious head in various areas of Celeste's life, but after losing her pregnancy, it seemed to sprout all the more. Pregnancy loss is a prime target for feelings such as these to emerge in spades. The lack of cultural discourse surely doesn't help. Celeste felt alienated, isolated, and, most especially, ashamed by the dissolution of her pregnancy. After the loss, she found it even harder—impossibly hard—to connect with her partner, and people more generally, for fear of being fully known, since at the core of it, she believed she was bad.

Of course, there are multiple ways in which shame manifests itself post-pregnancy loss. One instance that is rarely discussed, but that I see often in my practice, is the shame that occurs when a woman does not feel sad about her miscarriage but instead experiences relief, gratefulness, or simply no profound feeling at all. While our society has long demanded those who've experienced pregnancy loss grieve in silence, it should be noted that the grief is also usually an expected, required component. Women should want to be pregnant. Women should want to *stay* pregnant. And if they either cannot become pregnant or cannot stay pregnant, they should mourn the loss of this so-called vital cornerstone of womanhood. At least, that's what we're told.

For Marta, a thirty-three-year-old newlywed, it was the guilt of not feeling sad about her miscarriage she'd experienced ten years prior that brought her into my office. During the intervening years, she felt conflicted about *not* being conflicted. She felt a pressure, one that emanated from culture, to be attached to the idea of having a baby even though she didn't want to have one then. Now financially stable and in a healthy relationship, she wanted to build a family—to no avail. After two losses and one failed round of IVF, she began to wonder if her feelings of relief about her lost pregnancy a decade earlier had come back to haunt her. Were her struggles to conceive "karmic retribution," she speculated aloud to me, for being grateful her body had saved her a trip to the local Planned Parenthood, where she had intended to have an abortion? Was her current plight a divine decree, proof from a force far greater than her that there was something innately wrong with her for not wanting to carry a pregnancy to term all those years ago? Not being able to get pregnant now, her mind led her to rewrite a narrative she felt comfortable with up until this point. Now, with a wanted pregnancy seemingly unattainable, she searched for meaning in past events and assigned retaliation where there was none.

"Maybe if I had felt badly then I would be pregnant now," she said, unable to control her tears as they carved rivers down her face. "But I didn't feel badly then. And I don't feel badly about it now. I really don't. The truth is: I was so relieved that my body knew what my mind had figured out instantly—I wasn't ready to be a mom. And now that I am ready, this happens? This feels like a twisted joke. This feels like a punishment."

The idea that a miscarriage is a punishment for a past "misdeed" is common. The loss happened because the woman ate something. Lifted something heavy. Went to work. Slept on her right side. Slept on her left. Historically felt mixed feelings about becoming a mother. And given Marta's plans to terminate her unwanted pregnancy, it's unlikely that she would have been spared these present-day feelings of shame and guilt if she had not had a miscarriage, but the abortion as planned.

"What do you imagine your life would have been like

had you not miscarried ten years ago and carried that pregnancy to term?" I asked, shifting the focus to the undeniable aspects of Marta's story—the valid reasons why a pregnancy, at that time, wasn't ideal for her. And why one would be now.

She paused briefly, looking down at the tear-soaked tissue she had been fidgeting with in her lightly freckled hands. And it was then that I noticed an obvious shift in her physical demeanor. She looked back up at me and held my gaze.

"I wouldn't be who I am today," she said, almost defiantly. "There's no way I would have been able to finish school or end up at the job I have now. I wouldn't have met my husband. It's so hard to imagine what motherhood would have been like for me then, when I was in a less than ideal relationship with someone who was as ill-prepared to become a parent. I wasn't equipped, emotionally and otherwise, either. I wasn't ready. I just wasn't."

Once Marta began trying to get pregnant and couldn't, she eventually wondered if something about her was defective. Just like Celeste, she felt like a failure.

...

Attributing a miscarriage—and any response to it—to a personal character flaw or individual choice, rather than the basic comingling of chromosomes during fertilization and the profoundly unique ways in which we emotionally digest the happenings of our bodies, keeps us suspended in the past. In the absence of forgiveness and grace, understanding and ownership, self-blame and self-hatred are left to fester, causing far too many of us to relive these experiences and our responses to them over and over again. *What could I have done differently? How did I let this happen? What if I had done X instead of Y, Y instead of Z? Should I have felt this way instead?* And unfortunately, positioning a pregnancy loss as a moral or personal failing is something I hear about all too often in the context of both my work and my online community. This sentiment is prevalent in research as well.[16]

If we believe it is standard to get pregnant and stay pregnant, we are more apt to experience shame, as we believe our experience is somehow outside of the norm. If we believe there is one response to the loss of a pregnancy, and we do not embody that response, we are also more apt to experience shame, as we assume those we express our feelings to will judge us for not living up to society's expectations. Shame isn't just the logical conclusion, then, but actually serves to *reignite* silence and stigma. It encourages a sense that we, alone, are feeling this way. Why share it with others? Why reveal ourselves to be vulnerable in that way? And so, the cycle begins anew.

If shame is where the trifecta regenerates, it's also the best entry point to begin to break the cycle apart. As Brené Brown aptly put it, the antidote to shame is empathy.[17] Miscarriage means many things to many people; I wouldn't posit that there is any one defining feeling of a pregnancy-loss experience. But the best way to make room for all those experiences, for all those individual stories, is by speaking them aloud. Free from the all-too-pervasive trifecta. We may, for example, witness a sea change if we rebel against the notion that we should keep pregnancies "secret" until the second trimester, when we are "out of the woods." That way, we may begin to see loss as "normal" (or at least common), and in doing so, break down those often-reported feelings of alienation and isolation.[18] If we know we're not alone, suddenly we're not so stigmatized. If we know we're not alone, we can begin to chip away at that shame, letting it wriggle out of the isolating confines of our psyches, eventually fizzling out entirely as it languishes without a host to prey on. And if we could manage to do that, to squash shame when it threatens to overtake us, we can aim to ensure that future generations will be self-possessed when it comes to this topic. That they will know—and deeply believe—that their losses have absolutely nothing to do with something they did or didn't do. They will not hate on themselves. Period. That's the world I want to live in. That's the world I'm humbly hoping to help create.

# 4

*"I was understanding grief from a corporeal—*
*not simply a theoretical—perspective."*

Four years before my miscarriage, Penelope sat across from me in my sunlit office, shadowed in grief. She'd been trying to get pregnant for years, and had been coming to see me for nearly all of those. Her hair changed from one radical style to another, with alternating showstopping color combos. She liked change, or at least the kind that can be expressed externally. I saw her through it all. After three miscarriages and two unsuccessful IVFs, she spoke softly of her strained marriage, wringing her hands in her lap. I shifted my weight from one leg to the other, listening intently; she shifted her eyes toward the window. But no amount of diversion could hide what sat between us: my unmistakably pregnant belly.

Understandably, my patients wanted to know about my pregnancy with Liev; a third entity had entered the consultation room, altering the therapeutic dynamic. They peppered our sessions with questions like, "How do you feel?" (especially during the first trimester, when I glowed olive green) and, "Do you know if you're having a boy or a girl?" (I didn't). They wondered aloud how my impending motherhood would affect my work life. Some expressed concern I might not return to work. And even if I did, would I be able to see them, would I keep a similar schedule, work into the evenings like I had been? Others shared their complex and diverging feelings about returning to see me once I became a mother myself. They worried that my foray into motherhood might trigger their own loss histories so much that starting anew with another therapist might just be a less fraught route. I listened. I empathized.

My first pregnancy had come fast and was a remarkably simple time. I had no real concerns, no preoccupations. My husband and I traveled internationally, prepared our home to accommodate a third family member, and readied our careers the best we knew how. I called upon friends and family for tidbits of wisdom, hoping they would paint a candid picture of what was in store. For whatever reason, I wasn't overly concerned about the birth, breastfeeding, or even the inevitable sleep deprivation. Until those moments actually happened, I was in a hearty state of denial about the upcoming transformation and what it might do to my lifestyle.

Before pregnancy and throughout it, I worked long days seeing patients. I love my work, and my body seemed on board with maintaining this schedule as the pregnancy progressed. Folding motherhood into my already busy clinical and writing life felt initially daunting, especially as I began to map out my maternity leave. The closer it got, however, the clearer I became about how I ideally wanted to divide my time: three very full days at work, two days at home.

And so, in that session, I was feeling strong, confident. But Penelope, in her usual thoughtful tone, expressed concern that I would lose the pregnancy and pressed me for details about my status and symptoms. "Thank you for checking in," I'd respond. "I feel okay." Then I'd turn the focus back to her. Together we explored the feelings my pregnant belly evoked for her: her envy of my seemingly easy go of it, her fear that my pregnancy would end badly, her fantasy that my being a specialist in reproductive health somehow made me "immune"—that "probably nothing bad would happen" to me.

My son Liev was born that winter.

...

Traditional psychoanalytic theories envision the therapist as a blank slate on which patients project their thoughts and fantasies, a distant expert interpreting the patient from behind an inscrutable facade. Patients' concerns are seen as problems the doctor can "fix" through psychological suturing. Contemporary psychoanalytic viewpoints, by contrast, have given rise to a very different understanding of the therapeutic alliance, one in which the relationship *itself* is ultimately what's curative. But the therapist's quasi-anonymity remains a central tenet. Patients might inquire about a therapist's personal life, but unless it benefits the patient's growth to answer the question directly, the therapist usually explores what the question means to the patient.

I was originally drawn to the field of psychology as a young girl. In fact, looking back, it seems I was enacting a kind of mock group therapy with my dolls during imaginative play, ever since the fledgling age of five. I'd arrange my stuffed animals around the perimeter of my bed, all of them facing one another in a circle. I would invite the animals to share about their days, discuss books, concepts, and most especially, feelings. An interesting preview of what was to come, I suppose.

Flash forward to my late teens, early on in my college career, when I was introduced to Carol Gilligan's ground-breaking book *In a Different Voice*. This revolutionary piece of writing ignited a fire in me—one that set me ablaze on a path to pursue the study and practice of psychology, with a focus on girls and women's development. Gilligan's work zeroed in on making women's voices heard, in their own right and with their own integrity, for virtually the first time in social-scientific theorizing about women. Its impact was immediate and continues to this day. Her work has inspired new research, new educational initiatives, and political debate.

Gilligan believes that the field of psychology has persistently and systematically misunderstood women—their motives, their moral commitments, the course of their psychological growth, and their view of what is important in life. She set out to correct psychology's misperceptions and refocus its views on the psychology of women. A tour de force, Gilligan's perspective spoke to me on a fundamental level and set the stage for my vision of a career that took on these vital issues. With a passionate interest in community issues on both a minor and mass scale, I initially pursued a master's degree in public health, with a focus on international women's health and an aim of incorporating global perspectives on sexual and reproductive health, international health policy, pregnancy, and access to maternal healthcare. After several years of working in the field of public health locally and abroad—in Nigeria, Senegal, India, Nepal, and elsewhere—I was offered the opportunity to study directly with Carol Gilligan at Harvard University. An opportunity I couldn't pass up.

To have the chance to study under the very person who founded the field and spearheaded research on moral development specific to women was, in no uncertain terms, a dream come true. I was giddy with excitement and gratitude over how this was all coming to fruition. It was then that I had the chance to really integrate all of my academic and career interests—merging my studies of global reproductive issues with the psychology of women and girls. After completing my doctoral degree—which ultimately granted me the opportunity to work one-on-one with the very population of women on their paths to parenthood whom I'd been interested in for decades—I started taking patients.

Over the years, my patients have asked me a variety of personal questions focusing on a number of topics: my age, my marital status, my satisfaction in my marriage, my family history, my mental-health history, even. Of course, they are curious—how could they not be?—but some have pressed more than others. Questions like these often reflect dilemmas around trust, how they experienced maternal love in their early lives, emotional intimacy, deep-seated shame, and their aspirations for brighter, more stable futures. I should say that even I am subject to these lines of thinking: I was aware that my own therapist, Valerie, had been pregnant once. She had no children, though. She'd never volunteered more than the basics, but I was curious, figuring she'd be such a devoted mother, given how warm she was in our sessions. And so, I asked. "I wanted children and was pregnant, but it didn't work out for us," she shared. I wanted to know more, but we left it at that.

Like Valerie, I temper my reaction based on my understanding of the individual asking the question. For some, answering directly can be incredibly helpful, even healing. For others, though, it is best to proceed with caution. I share when I think it will be helpful and decline when I don't. The last thing I want to be is yet another person who adds to my patient's layered, internalized shame through shutting them down. But I also don't want to overstimulate them by disclosing information that may throw them off course in any number of ways, like comparing their lives to mine or taking up their therapy time with personal details that may create more of a disconnect than a bridge. It's a fine line, and I see it as my job to hold their histories and their growth at the core of my decision-making. When I think that a question might lead us into areas that are not ultimately helpful, I sensitively bring us back to the here and now.

So, when my body changed shape and my protruding belly filled the consulting room, the traditional therapeutic construct got turned on its head. Pregnancy is seen as a community event—strangers reaching for the belly, predicting the baby's sex, and even dispensing parenting advice. A woman's value while pregnant is reduced to the shape and size of her body, even more than normal. The intimacy of therapy provides a ripe opportunity to comment all the more, making it that much harder to escape these exchanges. Pregnancy asserts the therapist's presence and shatters her privacy in a way that nothing else does. I had no road map for it—none of my colleagues had so much as mentioned that this might happen, particularly my colleagues who had never been put in a position remotely like this, where the inclusion of their personal lives was unavoidable. My baby bump represented different things to different patients: an active sex life, a certain relationship status, a desire to raise a family. People pondered these elements of my life aloud, especially as the weeks pushed on and my body morphed; it became a very central part of the therapy sessions. And as my patients often told me, it stimulated longings that stemmed from their own maternal lineages.

• • •

Upon my return to work after my maternity leave with Liev, interactions with patients who'd mentioned struggling with my baby bump seemed to resume quite effortlessly, now that the visible reminder of my pregnancy had dissipated. We revisited their expressed feelings and made sure to sensitively acknowledge the transition that occurred in my personal life, which invariably affected my work life. But the newly established rhythm of working three full days and spending the others with my son felt mostly effortless.

So there was no reason for me to think my ability to merge my personal and professional life would in any way be altered by another pregnancy. I figured, *I've done this once before, surely I can do this again.* In fact, the ease of my pregnancy with Liev and my ability to navigate the subsequent "work-life balance" factored heavily in my decision to have another child. *I could do this.* Of course, there was no way for me to know that I would only be pregnant for four short, albeit physically uncomfortable, months. I had no idea that at the very moment when it would become physically obvious to my patients that I was pregnant, that pregnancy would cease to exist.

I emailed my patients to inform them that I'd lost the pregnancy and rescheduled their sessions. In writing, I assured them I was okay and that I looked forward to seeing them the following week. But when I returned, I was inundated by questions. I answered almost always in concise yet honest detail. I didn't want to incite fright; I also didn't want to be dishonest. "So you mean you went to your regular checkup at sixteen weeks and there was no heartbeat?" I felt compelled to reply candidly, "No, that's not how it happened. The baby actually fell out while I was at home. The day before, the heartbeat was there and everything looked fine."

I wondered how the change in my physical and mental presence would be experienced by my patients. Penelope, for one, chose not to return to therapy for a while. She said that my second-trimester miscarriage was a real-life manifestation of her "biggest nightmare." "If a later pregnancy loss happened to you," she explained, "it means it could happen to me."

Processing this particular type of trauma was not something I had learned about en route to completing my doctorate. Even the textbooks that I'd read about pregnancy complications—the medical ones, the psychological ones— never mentioned the therapist—*her* pregnancy—or how to address within the therapeutic dyad her obvious loss of a pregnancy. I would have to learn this as I went along.

I speculated that my miscarriage might potentially strengthen some of my patient interactions, because I now understood their grief from a corporeal, and not simply a theoretical, perspective. But I also recognized that my miscarriage might accentuate my vulnerability in ways that could hinder the therapeutic process. Would my patients be inhibited from freely discussing what might now, in the face of my fresh pain, seem like mundane details of their daily lives? I feared that they might want to protect me, comfort me, run from me, or shield themselves from my anguish, if only to fortify themselves against their own.

And they did. I felt uncomfortably center stage. Though I continued on in my empathy, I was invariably bogged down by my life, my loss, my all-too-pervasive grief. Some of my patients were forthcoming about the fears my loss provoked: "I had never really considered you as someone that bad things could happen to." "What if you had died? Then what of *me*?" Another common refrain: "If you're grieving, how will there be space for my grief here too? How can you support me if you are presumably in need of support yourself?" I needed time and space to deliberate each question, valid in its own way. We addressed their concerns each time they arose. Like grief, their newfound articulated fears of *my* humanness—*their* therapist's vulnerability—deserved keen attention and the inevitable softening of time.

In juxtaposition, other patients picked up where they left off in their previous sessions, resuming reflection on their own lives, seemingly unscathed by my sudden absence from the office and lack of a bulging belly. The truth is, though, I will never really know if they (consciously or even unconsciously) inhibited themselves for my sake. Personally, I felt zero judgment as they shared their struggles, of course, and was relieved to focus on someone other than myself as my body and mind reconfigured without a baby. But it was impossible for me not to contemplate the very real possibility that they were caught up in worrying about me, and perhaps to the detriment of their own therapeutic process. I invited them to share anything on their minds, most especially questions or concerns about my abrupt and recent change in pregnancy status, and in the end I have to trust my patients in the same way they trust me—I must err on the side of credence. I will likely never know what went on (if anything) in the context of their minds when I returned less poised, less like myself, less pregnant. I might never know if they even noticed.

Penelope eventually returned to my office, newly pregnant. In one session near the end of her first trimester, she paused in silent reverie—and then whispered, "I'm worried that what happened to you will happen to me."

I reassured Penelope that fear was inevitable, especially when it is tethered to a previous loss—grief knows no timeline, and one pregnancy does not erase the loss of another. With glassy eyes and a deep sigh, she said that hearing me talk about my residual worries eased the sense of isolation that surrounded her miscarriages, allowing her to feel less alone. She was growing less afraid of losing again.

...

Several months later, I got pregnant again, for a third time. The beginning of this pregnancy coincided with Penelope's last trimester. I, like Penelope, was now angst-ridden and plagued with uncertainty, despite evidence that the baby was healthy. This time around, Penelope seemed particularly attuned to my eyes. "You look worried," she'd say tenderly, her concern for me seemingly eclipsing even her own worries about giving birth. She was perceptive. My worry was indeed ever present. Each trip to the bathroom between patients included checking for blood: evidence of potential demise. Each morning, I reflexively went through a checklist of pregnancy symptoms, scanning my body to be sure that this pregnancy was holding fast. And I practically held my breath as I lay on the exam table awaiting each and every ultrasound, expecting the worst.

"I am worried," I would tell Penelope, honoring the trust we had long established within the confines of those four walls. "Pregnancy after pregnancy loss can be exhausting on so many levels. Loss has a way of stealing surrender." My therapeutic instincts had changed—mostly in the months following my miscarriage and through my subsequent pregnancy—and I wasn't necessarily confident for the better. But this was where I was. Speaking a bit more openly felt inevitable and somewhat refreshing, and according to my gut, was the best way to assist Penelope in her continued journey. This was uncharted territory, to be sure, but it felt foreordained. This was where I was supposed to be. This was what I was supposed to share. While Penelope's fears eased, I continued, very pregnant, to hear agonizing stories detailing a slew of pregnancy complications from other patients—complications I was all too aware could befall me. My patients and I had now strayed far from a pristine therapeutic dyad. We haphazardly made our way through a maze of human emotions. In sessions, I found myself reflexively saying "I understand how that feels" without considering how revealing these moments of solidarity truly were. I silently underlined comments I heard, shocked at how similar they were to thoughts that had entered my own mind.

Being pregnant—twice, in short succession—took its mental and physical toll. When I gave birth to my healthy daughter Noa Raye the following December, I took a much-needed maternity leave. I wept when I returned to my office, not because I struggled with the necessity of returning to work sans child, but because, following so many anxiety-laden months, my body still needed another release. It had safely brought my daughter into the world, but the overwhelm that grew inside me and along with her had remained. Going back to work, in a way, was another birth. Another transformation. Another beginning. No longer preoccupied with a pregnancy I felt could go wrong at any moment, I felt a sense of renewal and a sturdiness that I hadn't substantially embodied in over a year. I was more fully there, deeply present. I had missed this. I had missed me.

When I was back at work, a new patient, Maya, came to see me. She was ten weeks pregnant. Fifteen minutes into her first session, while describing sleepless nights filled with fear about becoming a parent, she paused, glanced at my bookcase, and then looked back at me: "Can I ask: Are you a mother?"

There was a time when I would have reflexively asked Maya what my maternity might mean to her. But instead, I considered revealing a small but profound piece of my life. I had changed. The "before" and "after" marked by my loss did not sequester itself to my personal life; it had altered my identity as a mental health provider too. And that transition—that subtle but marked shift in how I viewed therapy within the confines of my own trauma, and the newly discovered ability for that trauma to be discussed in a way that validated my patients' fears without overshadowing them—landed me somewhere between being a blank slate and the focal point of any therapeutic relationship. I had discovered a much more ideal middle ground.

"Yes," I told Maya. "I have two children."

## 5

*"If only it could have continued on this way."*

Talking to my patients about my miscarriage got easier. I was practiced, and could easily guide conversations away from myself, forever focused on the primary reasons for these visits and my role as facilitator, not the focal point. Talking to people in my personal life, however, seemed to grow more muddled at every turn.

In those initial hours following my loss, I was barely able to cobble together a coherent sentence, and couldn't imagine mustering the emotional energy it would've required to reach out to everyone individually, those closest to me that I had not been able to include in my frantic text. Still, I knew I had to tell people. So I settled on a group email. I figured it was best to share the news while it remained fresh, so people wouldn't inadvertently trigger me by asking how pregnancy was going, how I was feeling, how far along I was, whether I had a name picked out. Those common inquiries can be emotional landmines for anyone who has experienced a loss, and I set out to avoid the impending minefield entirely.

Chronicling the details of that day, abbreviated though they were, ended up being surprisingly cathartic. There was a peace that accompanied being able to reach out to those around me who needed to know what had transpired in a way that was contained. I also found relief in the ability to protect myself from the possibility that I would have to share my story before I was ready; that a well-meaning friend or family member, innocently asking about my pregnancy or how I was feeling, would blindside me. In dispersing the details of my miscarriage in a way that best suited me, I was discovering new parts of myself in real time as I made my way through this written reflection on my brief pregnancy.

Midway through the second paragraph of my email-turned-novella, I wrote:

*I know this may sound unexpected—weird, even—but somehow I have this deep-seated feeling that I trust my body now more than ever before. How can this even be? Surviving the birth process at home alone brought out this uncanny, almost animalistic ferocity in me, both psychologically and physically. It's what was required. What this inexplicable experience has driven home is that this now bleeding, empty body of mine—a body pregnant only hours ago—works. I inherently believe this. I'm not sure if this feeling will morph or be maintained, but right now I feel a sense of categorial trust. My body did not fail; it did its job, as painful as this dissolution may be.*

Looking back, I think my writerly inclination that evening was powered purely by adrenaline. Once I got started, it was hard to stop. Writing has that way about it for me. In an attempt at fending off dreaded questions by preemptively addressing the intricate details, I was not only acknowledging and attempting to assuage people's fears—I was acknowledging and fortifying myself from my own. But borne out of necessity was a reprieve I didn't realize I needed until it overcame me. This email, in essence, acted as a temporary lifeline as I sifted through the horror of my pregnancy gone wrong; getting it all out on paper and intimately evaluating the range of emotion flooding my weary body rang powerful.

This email also served as a kind of invitation for my loved ones—an invitation into this enervated chapter of my life. A chapter on death, and life after.

And so, the writing continued. I just couldn't seem to steal myself from the page once I got going.

*There are these wild, fleeting moments when my heart seems to literally expand—perhaps a dogged appreciation for my own survival and for the shape of my life; backed up against moments of irreparable shatter, my own heart still technically beating whilst feeling anything but viable, convinced emotional resuscitation will never be. Trauma seems to provoke this dichotomy, this corporeal confusion, as it were. It's both: gratitude for what is and utter despair for what isn't (and what could have been).*

I clicked Send.

With the tap of a key, off went my accidental sermon—about life, death, the liminal spaces in between—to those who didn't yet know. Straightaway, the love rushed in. Expressions of shock and compassion in equal measure. I was awed by the benevolent responses to this requiem on the loss of my pregnancy as I lay there bleeding, reading their words as my phone lit up with each reply, thanking my lucky stars for the privilege of having such a tender cadre of loved ones who would see me through what would no doubt be a dark, if not the darkest, period of my life.

...

One of the early responses that made my heart swell was from my wise-beyond-his-years younger brother, writing from Tel Aviv, where he was barreling through medical school:

*Dear Jess,*

*Let me start by saying that I have so much love and admiration for you. I hope you remember through the most trying times that you have so many people that love you and care for you.*

*I can't imagine what you have gone through these past many hours and what you continue to experience now. I am so sorry that you had to go through such trauma. I don't know how anyone could stay calm through such an ordeal.*

*Since there is no advice or consolation I can give that will make things better, I'll just tell you that I'm glad you are okay. I hope you are recovering physically and that you are comfortable now.*

*Please know that I am here for you. Such a silly, trite expression, but I really am. You can call me any time, and I mean that. If you even slightly want to talk, don't be shy. I'll be a willing ear. And don't feel pressured to talk to me, either. When you feel ready.*

*I wish more than anything that I could just give you a big, long hug. You and Jason. Please share this with him, if you like. My words apply to both of you. I love you both.*

*Always look forward to the future. It's going to be great.*

*Tons of love,*
*David*

If only these initial life preservers of support were enough to buoy me through the future waves of grief and mourning. If only the timeline of grief adhered to society's limited understanding of it, lasting a short period then vanishing under a sea of lovingly premade meals and kind sympathy cards and a few whispered tales of solidarity. If only my brother's words were enough. If only it could have continued on this way.

• • •

Within a matter of days, it was time to leave the house; to drop off Liev at school, take him to swim class, go on play-dates. What choice did I have? My head was topsy-turvy and I felt anything but poised for these meetups, but I wanted to keep Liev's life running as usual, so I showered, dressed, threw on lipstick, even, and headed out into the world.

I braved it. A world that had spinned madly on as I endured the worst trauma of my life. A world that had simply maneuvered around me that fateful day on the sidewalk, when I clutched the plastic bag holding the remains of my daughter and squeezed the blood-soaked towels between my thighs. A world that doesn't much like talking about miscarriage, let alone a baby dying and falling out of your body in your home. I didn't feel like I belonged to this world. I didn't believe this world wanted to belong to me.

My forlorn body—on display as I ventured into requisite pleasantries at preschool pickup—slumped as I said my hellos. Still bleeding and required to wear a clunky pad, I felt like a teenager again—a gawky stranger in my own skin, confused by a body I didn't fully understand. Excruciating reminders of what was and then what wasn't, and also, what definitely shouldn't be: belly hollowing, hormones blazing, blood continuing. Smiling fellow-mom acquaintances uttered niceties—the usual hellos and how are yous—as, unbeknown to them, the aftereffects of my loss ravaged my should-be pregnant body.

In more ways than one, I was still stuck on that sidewalk, shouting the details of my loss to my sister over the phone as people simply carried on around me. This time, it was my body shouting. In pain. In anguish. In anger. Soon, my voice would follow.

$$\cdots$$

As I not-so-gingerly shared my story with other friends, family, and random people who remembered I was pregnant, I increasingly became more stunned by the reactions—the actions and inactions of people around me. All I yearned for were authentic yet simple pleasantries. Even just a plain "How are you feeling?" would suffice. Four words. Nothing more. Instead, I heard variations on "You're so strong, you'll be fine. You'll get through this."

I didn't want pity or saccharine sympathy, of course. And I certainly didn't want to enter into a trauma-off, which so often seemed to be the outcome—women comparing their loss stories to mine. Examples abound, but there's one in particular that sticks out: A woman I didn't know messaged me on Instagram following her scheduled D&C to extract a pregnancy she lost at eight weeks. She said something to the effect of, "My D&C went smoothly. It was not as big of a deal as I thought it would be at all. I went to sleep; didn't feel a thing. Woke up and it was done. Just like yours but two months earlier." I was taken aback and naturally thought that she must've messaged the wrong person. But she didn't. She meant to reach out to me.

It was a human mistake, of course, to assume our experiences were similar. But it alerted me yet again to the ways in which we reflexively compare and contrast loss experiences—an outcome of our painfully inadequate understanding of death, grief, and trauma. Because in the absence of understanding, it seems, we're left to rely on the context of our own experiences, and often make the mistake of using what we've endured as a way to gauge what we believe other people should endure as well. The common refrain is "I made it through this, so you can too." What is meant to come off as support is in actuality dismissive.

Let's aim to refrain from assumptions and, most especially, from minimizing or magnifying these grief-stricken journeys. I've seen this so many times in my office, women saying some variants of: "I feel like I should be over my loss by now. I was only six weeks along. It could have been so much worse." "At least it was early." "At least I know I can get pregnant." "At least my milk didn't come in." "At least I didn't feel the baby move." "At least I wasn't overly attached." "At least my grieving process won't go on and on like theirs might." "It feels indulgent to feel this." It's a base impulse, to compare, but it really doesn't serve anyone. Why does it matter whose suffering is "worse"? And is this even a *thing*, comparing and contrasting pain? Pain is pain. Grief is grief. Incalculable at their best, sadistic at their worst, pregnancy outcomes surely don't lend themselves to a discrete or linear hierarchy. No one wants to find themselves atop a mountain of pain, shouting, "I win! My loss is the worst-possible scenario. Worse than yours and yours and also yours!"

With patients, I used—and still use—a careful response: "Your pain is just as real and valid and important as anybody else's. Your loss matters because it is your loss. Your hope, dashed. Your body, grieving. Your sadness. Your love. Try to resist the urge to compare and contrast. There needn't be a loss/grief hierarchy. It only serves to minimize your experience. Face your pain without distracting it by somehow making it less than. Or too much. You are significant. Your heart is shattered. Lean into the ache. It's yours." Within the safety of my practice, I felt comfortable parsing out this innate reaction to pain and loss more thoroughly. I could push back on the notion that one's level of grief needn't be dictated by another's, especially because in doing so I was also doing my job.

But in my personal life, I felt like I had no choice but to stem the tide and cut off these types of conversations. Instead of wading into vulnerable territory to disprove the belief that our traumas must be measured against the size and significance of someone else's, I amped up my boundaries, repeating my own version of the "I'm good" refrain, somewhat defensively: "I wasn't even sure I wanted a second child anyway." "I was terrified to raise a girl in this culture." Probably my most frequent utterance was "I'm okay, really."

But just as I'd seen countless times before—yet somehow still wasn't prepared for in my own life—the sticky tendrils of my trauma began to strangulate. Flashbacks, numbness, avoidance, sweat-soaked night terrors, anxiety, hypervigilance—you name it. Berated by a cacophony of discordant thoughts, I was officially rendered compassless.

And though I'd heard from patients about the unintentional and seemingly universal horror of platitudes, navigating this firsthand was another thing entirely. Some conversations were smooth, others stilted, some not half-bad. I wasn't sure what to make of the disappointments, the strained face-to-face interactions at preschool drop-off, the awkward pauses with friends I'd been close with for decades. Each a sucker punch to the gut.

Some subtle, others demonstrative, these blows hurled me into elaborate fantasies of intermittent hiding. But I had to resist; I had to push on.

• • •

I figured I'd huddle up close to those I'd known the longest. After all, they knew me—and I knew them—best.

So I set out to meet up with Sara. While Sara has never lost a pregnancy, she has lost people close to her, and she is one of my dearest childhood friends. We met in the fourth grade and have remained close ever since—ski trips to Mammoth, cross-country visits during college, long phone calls about our respective crushes, career ambitions, budding sex lives. She has a heart of gold and that wit of hers brings me to my knees in belly laughter every time. I knew she'd throw her arms around me and her embrace would remind me of the person I was before this horrendous experience. A person I so desperately missed.

Even though my anxiety was nearing an unparalleled level, I didn't want to let myself reschedule our lunch plans. I knew seeing her would be good for my soul and that catching up face-to-face might rejuvenate me. I let her know in advance that my anxiety was at an all-time high—9.75 out of 10, to be exact. I wanted to give her a heads-up on my unfortunate labile state, to give her the opportunity to cancel in case my mourning was too overbearing. She was still up for it.

I arrived early. She was ten minutes late. I didn't feel well. I thought about leaving. I waited.

She showed up in a turquoise A-line dress with gray side-zip booties and a trio of beaded gold, silver, and copper necklaces. She looked effortless as she floated toward me; her joie de vivre lit up her dark-brown eyes adorned in elongating mascara, with just a puff of blush illuminating her pale, porcelain cheeks. I envied the feeling she emanated. It was so good to see her. It had been a while. But it was hard too. Seeing her in her natural vitality underscored how desolate my insides felt, how downtrodden I must have looked. Connecting with someone who knew me when I was full of life mirrored back to me just how low I'd sunk.

As we picked at our salads, we talked about stuff going on in her work life, our kids, and the anxiety I'd been confronted with ever since my miscarriage. "Do you want to see a photo of the baby?" I ventured. "I know it's intense, but I wondered if you might want to see what I saw; if you'd like to see her." Sara's eyes glazed over with empathy. "Of course I want to see her. I can't believe you have photographs." I grabbed my phone, opened the camera roll, and clicked on one of the images taken that day as I lay on the table during the D&C. I felt thankful again that my midwife friend had had the presence of mind to snap these, knowing what an important vestige they'd be as I navigated my grief.

"NOOOOOO!" Sara screamed, not quite loud enough for other tables to hear, as she averted her wincing gaze from the fetus that fell from my body a couple of weeks prior. She looked disgusted. The mood plummeted. I felt horrid, like I'd done something wrong. I quickly found myself trying to make *her* feel better with a string of bumbling apologies as I awkwardly shoved my phone deep in my bag, as if to bury the evidence. I could feel my face warm with shame. Or maybe it was anger? Perhaps a commingling of both.

"I'm sorry. Should I not have shown that to you?" I muttered in an embarrassed, hushed tone, as if I'd somehow done something wildly inappropriate.

Encapsulated in a cloud of silence for what felt like an eternity, we sipped sparkling water, chewed chunks of ice, and avoided eye contact.

Things devolved from there.

In an attempt at a lighter note, Sara looked up from her now-empty water glass.

"You look svelte; as if you weren't even pregnant. Aren't those your prepregnancy J Brand jeans?"

Gulp. I gave a perfunctory nod. "Yeah, the baby weight came off almost overnight."

I could feel even my skin withdrawing from this seemingly frivolous direction of the conversation. From dead-baby photograph to the size of my body and jeans? *This can't be happening*, I thought to myself.

"Lucky you! That must be a relief."

*A relief that my baby died and that I don't look like I was ever pregnant? Please don't erase my pregnancy with a trivial remark about the shape of this body of mine*, I shouted in my head.

I calmly replied, "I guess."

Her attempt to redirect the conversation put us smack in another emotional minefield: Talking about women's bodies. Mine, specifically. People had said similar things to me after my son was born—"You look like you were never pregnant!"—and I found myself chafing against the declaration, which was so earnestly meant to be a compliment. I was, of course, changed. I *wanted* to be changed. I welcomed, was even overjoyed at, the physical and psychic changes brought about by motherhood. This moment was entirely different, but nonetheless the same. This pregnancy had left a mark on me; I didn't want to hear that Sara couldn't see it, or that it had been erased entirely. Also, I wished I were still pregnant, so hearing that I didn't look like I had *ever* been pregnant was no consolation at all. Everywhere I looked, I was boxed in by another conversation I did not want to have. Conversations I knew were intended to help, but which too often blatantly missed the mark.

Turning points happen when you least expect them, I guess. I learned this too well through the trauma of my loss, and here again, reiterated in love. This galling exchange stung to the core; and so, I licked my gaping wounds as I grew more anxious on my brief drive home, up into the placid hills, even more depleted than I had been two hours prior.

Sometimes—I found rather quickly—having history with someone doesn't necessarily protect you from egregious statements, unintended harsh comments, or unfortunate stalemates. Sometimes, instead, hearing afflictive words from someone you've known your entire life can be arresting, blanketing you in an isolation no one should ever know.

• • •

"Oh, the karma!" a family member exclaimed when I shared by phone that the bleeding, which had finally ceased, began to trickle once again. Blood spilling from my body once more: a continued consequence of the miscarriage. I didn't have the stamina to digest this misfire amid the reinjury I was navigating, as I riffled through my bathroom cabinet in search of yet another clunky pad. I thought I was done with these. Later, however, when I had a moment to think, I was effectively flattened by her off-handed insinuation. Was she implying that I somehow *deserved* this miscarriage and the subsequent, seemingly never-ending bleeding? That I had done something in my life that set me up for this grand devastation? Sucker punched once more, I felt the wind knocked out of me.

Questioning my own hurt feelings and my interpretation of this comment, I went to Google and looked up the formal definition of karma. Maybe it was me who didn't understand. In Hinduism and Buddhism, karma means "the sum of a person's actions in this and previous states of existence, viewed as deciding their fate in future existences. Destiny or fate, following as effect from cause."[19]

I was speechless as I mulled over what this utterance—
*Oh, the karma!*—signified about how this family member
of mine viewed me, life's trajectory, and perhaps, most
especially, spotlighted her conceptualization of tragedy.
Was she implying that my miscarriage was in some way
my fault, and my fault alone? A lesson I deserved to learn?
Something I'd done in my past now catching up with me,
something so abominable that I somehow had a hand in my
fate, now crushing my spirit? To make matters more confusing, had she suddenly adopted religious/cultural beliefs
outside of her own (Judaism) that she likely knew little, if
nothing, about? Did she fully comprehend the meaning of
the word "karma"? I couldn't make sense of it. The comment burrowed into my bones. It remains there. It festers
sometimes, still.

. . .

There were lots of little instances like this, off-handed
remarks burned into my mind with their (perhaps unintended) cruelty. Take the first Thanksgiving after my loss,
which featured a showstopping awkward moment when a
family friend excitedly shouted from across the table, "Con-
gratulations on your pregnancy!" It was six weeks after my
miscarriage. He hadn't heard that I'd lost the pregnancy.
Stunned, I calmly looked around the room to secure a
waiter to bring me a vodka tonic with a twist of lime, and
fast. In hushed tones, this uninformed friend was quickly
educated about my recent loss as I sipped my cocktail, now
tinged with tears.

The following day, Jason, Liev, and I boarded a plane

originally meant to take us on a celebratory "babymoon." Instead, with a hollow uterus and pulsating hormones and no baby to nurture, I had a sad week on a stunning beach.

While there, I thought, *Fuck it, I deserve some self-care.* A massage or two could ease the tension in this body of mine that had just been to hell and back. So I shuffled into the airy, lavender-infused spa, and lay still on a wooden table. I would have given anything to experience a sense of peace for even a few minutes.

"Anything specific going on in your body?" she asked.

*You can say that again,* I thought to myself. "Well, yeah, I lost a pregnancy at four months along recently."

She uttered words of sympathy and began to touch my tender body. Halfway through the treatment, as I began to feel the calm I'd been yearning for, she spoke.

"So, do you think there's something you did that caused your miscarriage?"

And just like that, on the precipice of peace, I was pulled back into war.

· · ·

In the wake of so many missteps—so many well-intentioned comments, questions, and regurgitated platitudes gone awry—I felt discombobulated. In an effort to try to carefully balance between my desire to retreat and regroup alone, and my acknowledged need to reach out and locate the arsenal of support that would no doubt flank me, I felt suspended in my grief: Do I risk bringing people into the fold who, like Sara, I believe could offer me the support I need? What if I, like I had been with Sara, was wrong? Could I handle another devastatingly awkward conversation about my jeans size? Could I weather another comment about my now nonpregnant body?

Turns out, the decision was somewhat made for me. Aside from a smattering of people—a handful of individuals from various parts of my life whose only commonality was showing themselves present, empathic and willing— the vast majority of people that I knew did not seem accessible. Those who did rush to my side were instrumental in my healing, eventually helping to restore me back to some patchwork version of who I'd known myself to be. But for everyone else, it seemed as though my unconscionable experience somehow forced them to flee.

*Where have they gone?* I wondered. I began to second-guess myself. After all, I was navigating wonky hormones, and my sensitivity was without a doubt on high volume; so I turned inward and asked myself: Was I misunderstanding something? Overthinking, maybe? Or were these friends of mine, both old and new alike, indeed reaching out to me with less frequency than they had prior to my loss?

My hunch was confirmed not long after by a dear friend of mine, who relayed the feelings a mutual friend of ours had expressed to her. It went something like this: My miscarriage triggered her own fears of losing her pregnancy, propelling her to avoid interacting with me when she could. Lacking any certainty of what exactly it was she should say to me, she opted instead to say nothing at all.

I get it: the fear of talking about the incomprehensible. We are human after all, and so it is understandable that we shy away from what the vast majority of us have labeled as "tough topics." But we must attempt to embody a sense of eagerness when it comes to those we love, those in our inner circle, and also, hopefully, our community at large. We at least need to try. To grasp at words, convey love, communicate care. Something. Anything. Anything other than silence, avoidance, or disappearing altogether.

...

As time passed, and I had conversations with patients and friends, it became increasingly clear that my miscarriage—and therefore I—was seen as some sort of contagion. People seemed to think that if they should dare get too close, they might be putting themselves at risk of experiencing what I'd gone through, or some semblance of it. And while to the objective mind that concept is obviously unfounded, it seems to be a permeating theme, dominating the thought processes of countless women who've been pregnant, who wrestle with the fear of loss, and who've seen firsthand what destruction grief leaves in its wake.

This story is, of course, not unique to me. Time and again, women have reported similar feelings of overwhelming isolation.

...

Alexandra spoke of these themes often during our weekly sessions together. At the customary twenty-week anatomy scan, she'd learned that her developing baby had a fatal heart condition, and was advised to terminate. Up until this point, there had been nothing alarming on ultrasounds, and the baby seemed perfectly healthy. Receiving this diagnosis meant her baby would not survive, let alone thrive. Plagued with guilt and a sense of alienation from her usual community, she talked about how alone she'd been navigating the choppy waves of grief, and described her inclination to hide the actual details of her story due to the unfortunate politicization of her so-called choice.

"Even my friends who've miscarried don't seem to understand. My friend who had a stillbirth at thirty-eight weeks doesn't seem to get me either. People think that because I got to *choose*, because I made a *decision*, my grief can't be anywhere near as overwhelming as theirs," Alexandra repeated each week as we discussed her disappointment and flagrant lack of support. She saw that in speaking her truth, she was met with people's judgment. And so, she opted to no longer talk openly about terminating, instead saying, "I lost the pregnancy," in an effort to steer clear of moral evaluation and earsplitting reactions. Unable to share the extent of her painful truth, her feelings festered.

She, too, was barraged by the usual platitudes, as so many women are: "At least you know you can get pregnant." "God has a plan." "At least you already have a healthy child." Perhaps most frequently, she was met with, "It just wasn't meant to be." These statements rang hollow for Alexandra, as they do for so many of us, so she searched for support high and low, in places previously foreign to her: message boards, Instagram accounts, a Facebook group for those in a similar situation, and here in therapy. It was difficult for her to find what she was looking for "out there." "Out there," support continued to come up short.

She berated herself aloud, wondering if she'd made the "wrong decision," if this somehow made her a "bad person," and if by making this "choice" she'd be "punished" and unable to get pregnant once again. She worried that people's judgment and lack of empathy were, in fact, justified. This worry of hers turned swiftly into rage, resentment, and harsh self-blame.

I've seen this time and again: disappointment from the outside internalized. I've watched as shame, stigma, and judgment whittle away at the resolve of those already in mourning, eventually overwhelming and manipulating the truth: That this is not their fault. That they did nothing wrong. Oftentimes, it is society at large's ignorance, indifference, or prosecutorial criticisms that lead us to believe our losses are our fault. A punishment we somehow deserved. Pain was accumulating. It was palpable. "Your grief is yours," I'd repeat. "You did absolutely nothing wrong. If this was a *decision*, you made a loving one. You deserve as much support as anybody else. You are entitled to your grief. It is yours."

Sometimes my words seem immediately absorbed, and I can watch via body language the relief envelop my patients. Other times, this mantra, as it were, is skimmed over or worse, outright rejected. And in those moments, I witness them clinging onto self-hating beliefs and gutting guilt, their bodies rigid with blame. I stay the course and meet them where they are, time and again, as they process what they've experienced and people's reactions to it. This is what support looks like. This is what we all deserve: to be buoyed no matter where we are.

To be heard. To be validated. To be nurtured. To be safe. To be steady.

These are the ways of support. You are entitled to your feelings. They are yours, and yours alone.

...

I think we are somehow conditioned to believe that grief is an evaluable property. That if we stack it up against others' experiences (or our own), we can determine how long and how strongly we—or they—ought to be grieving. Like there is some invisible point system, tallying what we are allowed to feel, how long we are allowed to mourn, whether we have met the minimum tragedy threshold to be allowed to ask for help. With pregnancy loss, especially an early one, you might find, for example, that people think it is not deserving of the same type of compassion we offer those who have lost a relative, or a friend. "Aren't you over it by now?" or "at least it happened early in the pregnancy. You'll move forward quickly" are two salient and all-too commonly spoken examples I hear about in my office from patients and in online conversations. Bombarded by crushing disappointment and disillusioned despair, women express how dumbfounded they are—having thought their loved ones were more capable of nuanced empathy than they showed themselves to be. It's as if the perceived severity of a loss situation somehow determines a grief time frame and its course, one that is delineated by others—others often being people who are not in the throes of it themselves.

But grief needn't be monitored or surveilled. Though one woman's loss might seemingly be "easier" or "harder" than somebody else's, we can't really know what her emotional experiences leading up to this point have been. One woman's six-week loss might be felt as a normative, expectable, and unemotional event, while another woman's six-week loss might yield complex ongoing grief. We can't know unless we inquire. We all bring our individual histories of loss, community, and support to current losses.

Next time you hear about a loss, try to remember that

one person's interpretation might be altogether different than the person's standing beside them. One woman might get pregnant "easily," another through IVF; another has suffered multiple losses, another already has many children but wants more, and another thought she never wanted to be a mother—the list goes on. No matter the specific details of what any one person is going through, we all benefit from loving support and the suspension of judgment.

• • •

Still, it is not easy to know what to say, a fact I understand. Scrambling to show compassion or to avoid putting our feet in our mouths can surely prove onerous. The following bit of guidance on what to say—and what not to say—after a loved one experiences pregnancy loss can hopefully change all of that.

*Don't say:* I haven't reached out because you seem fine. I thought it was better not to bring it up.
*Do say:* You can turn to me—to vent, weep, reflect. I'm here to listen.
    Some people prefer privacy, others long for support, or a little bit of both. Find out what she wants. Do not disappear. Challenge yourself to show up even if it makes you uncomfortable.

*Don't say:* At least you know you can get pregnant. Things will be different next time.
*Do say:* I'm sorry for your loss.
    Resist predicting the health of future pregnancies. Attempting to foresee like this minimizes what

just happened, how she's feeling in this moment, and assumes she will try again.

*Don't say:* My miscarriage wasn't as difficult as yours, mine happened early, in the first trimester.
*Do say:* This is a significant loss.

People start picturing their future families at different stages. Resist comparing trauma. Swapping stories might provide support—but it could just as likely create anxiety, envy, or resentment.

*Don't say:* At least you have a healthy child. You were ambivalent about having another baby anyway.
*Do say:* . . .

Say nothing about her future babies or current children. Now is not the time. Shame, guilt, and self-blame are common among women who miscarry. Bringing up her ambivalence could compound confusion.

*Don't say:* The baby wasn't healthy. Aren't you relieved things ended early? It wasn't really even a baby yet.
*Do say:* How have you been feeling since receiving the test results—since learning the baby wasn't healthy?

Millions of pregnant women miscarry every year. Despite the fact that miscarriage is common, many women who miscarry feel alone. Often, they're scared of what this loss might mean about their reproductive futures. This is not the time to debate what constitutes an embryo, a fetus, or a baby. Loss is real, no matter the time frame.

*Don't say:* You can always adopt.

*Do say:* I will not focus on "fixing" your future. I can be present with you in your pain.

Unless asked, do not give advice on family-building options. Let her lead the discussion about how she envisions her reproductive future.

*Don't say:* It wasn't meant to be. Everything happens for a reason.

*Do say:* Some people try to pinpoint a reason why their miscarriage occurred. You did nothing wrong. This is not your fault.

Support her in shying away from searching for things she might believe she's done to deserve or create this loss. A majority of miscarriages are a result of genetic issues.

*Don't say:* You look great! You don't even look like you were pregnant.

*Do say:* It's wonderful to see you. How are you feeling?

Commenting on her body, even if you are delivering what you think is a compliment, erases her recent pregnancy. This comment could also incite anger or disappointment that she's no longer pregnant.

*Don't say:* As soon as you get pregnant again, your grief will wane.

*Do say:* Time eventually eases sadness.

Some women grieve, others don't. We shouldn't assume miscarriage affects people in the same way or for the same amount of time. There is no benefit to rushing heartache.

I implore each of us to speak up—to talk about the very things that make us uncomfortable. To examine our fears, our superstitions, and our premonitions, if only as a way to understand what it feels like to engage rather than shut down when we find ourselves reckoning with an untimely death. Be present in no uncertain manner, and engage. If conversation about the vicissitudes of miscarriage became contagious, then the shame and isolation that often accompany this type of loss could, perhaps, be contained.

## 6

*"I don't know what I expected her to say,
but it wasn't that."*

I was born in the dry heat of August in New Mexico. My
father was working on the Laguna-Acoma Reservation
about fifty miles west of Albuquerque as a form of govern-
ment service following his medical training. His days were
full of caring for patients, and my mother spent most hours
of the day looking after a toddler (my sister) and a newborn
(me) on the reservation, about a mile down the road from
the clinic on Route 66.

Life events and pursuits ultimately led to differing
yearnings for my parents. I would not be surprised if the
strain of these circumstances contributed to the end of their
marriage. They met at a party a handful of years before my
older sister was born in Jerusalem in 1965 and married two
years later—just a few weeks before my dad started medical school—and I think it's safe to say they grew apart as
they each grew up. Our family moved to Los Angeles while
my father undertook his residency at UCLA. By the time I
was four years old my parents had split up, and my sister
and I lived with our mother, seeing our father on weekends

and Wednesdays. I have no concrete memory of my parents being married. I have no memory of their divorce.

My most vivid memories during my early childhood were the stretches of time between my father's visits. I remember Carly Simon and James Taylor blaring on the turntable in the living room, their gorgeous, plaintive voices wafting across the house while I anxiously waited for my dad to come get me.

$$\cdots$$

My father was the person I turned to when tweenhood commenced. When the time came, we discussed growing pains, breasts, pubic hair, menstruation, and fledgling boy crushes. I'm sure my girlhood ease in discussing such intimate things with my father was partly because he is a physician, but it was also because he took me seriously. He was matter-of-fact about the big questions of each successive milestone. He normalized these maturational seismic shifts just by being himself, and in doing so, validated my ability to be *myself*. His quick wit and deep, smiling eyes inspired certitude and steadiness, even while talking about ephemeral things like bras and girl gossip and tampons.

On the one-year anniversary of my miscarriage, my father's was the voice I wanted to hear. I sobbed on the phone, replaying the details to him as my very pregnant belly jiggled with new life. He wept, too, as we reflected on my pain and he described what it was like to hear his "baby" go through this traumatic loss. He said he admired my courage to enter pregnancy again and provided me with a resting place to lay my grief.

Two months later, my father came straightaway to

see me in the hospital after Noa was born on a drizzling night in mid-December. Watching him hold his brand-new granddaughter while he retold the story of my birth felt like something out of a movie. He recounted that long-ago night: how he and my mother had zoomed like the speed of light in their beige Volkswagen bus from the Laguna-Acoma Reservation to Presbyterian Hospital in Southeast Albuquerque. My dad likes to half-jokingly throw in that he thought he might have to deliver me in the back seat of the car because my mother's contractions were quickening and the van simply couldn't go any faster. He talked about my mom's unmedicated birth with me, just moments after my unmedicated birth with my daughter, and marveled at the passage of time and the awe that hangs in the balance.

• • •

"Oh my goodness, you still look pregnant!" my mother said, scanning my body up and down. It was two days after my miscarriage. I don't know what I expected her to say, but it wasn't that. I instantly regretted letting her visit while the trauma was still fresh.

My mother's comment landed with a dull thud. Her words felt like a critique, an admonishment. Why was she talking about my appearance?

The comment burrowed in me the same way my conversation with Sara did—this culturally mandated bad habit women have of reducing one another to our bodies' shapes and sizes, then calculating our worth based on these measurements. It rarely, if ever, makes us feel good, so why do we do it? Why do we persist in commenting on women's bodies—be they pregnant, unpregnant, post–pregnancy loss, or post pregnancy with baby? Why do we cling to this cultural obsession with women's bodies in times of duress, as if the size of our jeans can somehow mitigate the grief of a loss or smooth over the edges of trauma?

• • •

Was the obsession with my size my mother's way of deflecting the reality of the situation? Was she trying to distance herself from the suffering that was radiating off me in waves? It all just felt so . . . inadequate. I was overcome by disappointment and surprise, feelings I experienced in a multitude of ways in the aftermath of my miscarriage. An unwillingness or inability to confront the pain of what had happened. I felt it from loved ones and even some colleagues. But from my mother? Mothers are people we hope—dare I say expect—will love us wholly, protect us, know how to comfort us, and rush toward their children in moments of crisis, not avert their eyes or talk about body shape. Not rely on harmful messaging as a way to, inadequately, see us through trauma.

I didn't respond immediately, but the unintentional cruelty of my mother's comment sat with me all day. Unable to set it aside, I called her that evening hours after she'd left my house.

"What you said today really hurt my feelings," I blurted out when she answered. "Commenting on my body days after a miscarriage is completely inappropriate. I just lost a baby. At home, alone! I saw a dead baby! My dead baby."

My rational self knew that my words would probably be met with an impenetrable wall of bricks. But I was not in a rational state.

She was on the defensive immediately. "Oh, you are so sensitive, Jessica! I just never know how to get things right with you."

She hung up.

With the angry click of the phone, and the sound of nothing but a dull dial tone, my grief swelled. I burst into tears. This wasn't the first time I had been besieged by one of my mother's off-handed comments. This interaction, however, marked a turning point. For years, I made excuses for these kinds of exchanges. But this time, I expected—I needed—more. I couldn't unknow the decades of mother-daughter disappointment, just like I couldn't unknow the devastation of seeing my dead baby dangling from me.

I called back. She refused to speak to me. With my anxiety spiking, I persisted. I called again. Finally and reluctantly, she listened.

"Of course I still look pregnant, Mom! I wish I *were* still pregnant. How can you not see the cruelty in what you said?"

•••

The truth about that conversation is that it revealed many things. It wasn't just about my complicated relationship with my mother. It was a reflection of something more pervasive. In my many years of working with patients who had lost pregnancies, I understood on an intellectual level that our society wasn't equipped to deal with this topic, even among mothers and their daughters. But it wasn't until I was confronted with my own loss, and my own mother's inability to find the right words, that I felt the sting of our cultural inadequacies.

Months later, my mother and I revisited what happened between us. What I came to learn was that my mother had not known anyone who had miscarried—or, put more accurately, because of the silence around miscarriage, she wasn't aware that she knew anyone.

She hadn't been confronted with having to find the "right" words until now. Though her comment was unfathomable, it opened my eyes to a larger cultural issue: our lack of conversation surrounding miscarriage, stillbirth, and infant loss.

I was left to wonder if my mother—and others who have floundered in the face of this kind of trauma—would know what to say if we refused the current state of silence. I am not minimizing my mother's transgressions. Instead, I am calling for a cultural framework that aims to normalize, destigmatize, and provide tools for mothers and daughters (and others) to empathize more wholly.

I wish my mother had supported me differently after my miscarriage. My hope is that by attending to our cultural patterns of communication with regard to pregnancy loss, we will all have access to more loving, less fraught interchanges.

7

*"The body and failure become conflated.*
*It's a complicated coupling."*

Our bodies prepare for parenthood during pregnancy. Milk ducts swell. Bellies expand. The uterus rises. Muscles stretch. If that pregnancy is then lost, the next course of action is decided by the body, and the body alone. Depending on where we were in pregnancy, our bodies might take some time to fully comprehend and adjust to the nature of the loss. Milk arrives for a baby that did not. Hormones plunge us into the depths of the postpartum experience without an infant to serve as a breath of fresh air.

In my case, I don't know what I thought would come of my tender breasts, which had become swollen over the sixteen weeks of my pregnancy, but it shocked me to find them engorged with milk following my miscarriage. How is the body to know when "liquid gold" no longer has purpose—that it can't one day sustain the little being that no longer inhabits the womb? Our bodies don't know, until they know.

The unexpected sensation began as I was on a drive just two days after my miscarriage. I peeked under my shirt and into my bra as I felt my nipples abuzz. *What is going on?* I thought to myself. *Why are my breasts hard as rocks?* My breasts began to leak—milk streamed down my now-softening belly. There was no hungry newborn to receive it. No need for a pump to collect it. No point in lamenting its waste—who it was meant for was gone. Another unforeseeable layer of grief. Another reminder of what was and then what wasn't.

Of course, no one else saw me in that moment alone in my car. What the world around me saw instead was another choice my body made of its own volition: to rapidly shrink back to its prepregnancy state. Other people saw a woman who was, as Sara had pointed out, back in her prepregnancy pants just a few days later. I'll admit, I was genuinely troubled by how fast my prepartum body returned. It seemed not only odd but cruel—as if my body was trying to erase a pregnancy my mind hadn't yet let go of, even after my body had.

I suppose other people at the very least found my body's return to "normal" noteworthy as well—as it happened, Sara was not the only one who commented on my size. "You don't even look like you were pregnant," they'd say. And what they perceived was true. I didn't. But I still wanted to be. I assume these people thought they were saying something . . . *nice*? As if acknowledging my body had already rid itself of the physical evidence of a pregnancy that did not last would aid my mind in purging itself of its memory too. But their words hardly registered as a compliment. What people didn't see was how this speedy size change of mine added yet another dimension to my grief. Having been pregnant for four months and so suddenly having no outward evidence of that time seemed to erase for others the excruciating pain I was in. But I wanted proof. At the very least, I needed proof.

I wanted to *look* pregnant. I wanted to *be* pregnant.

•••

Sometimes women want to maintain their newfound pregnancy shape so much so that they mourn each and every crevice as it morphs into something else. They want to be pregnant still—to hold on to the form that housed a life for however long—and maintaining the size of a pregnant body becomes part of both the longing for a pregnancy that was lost and a vital part of the grieving process too. Shape change, another complex element of the bereavement process, can be poignant.

Keiko came to my office when she was freshly pregnant, at seven weeks along. She reported a recent rise in anxiety—steadily increasing ever since she peed on a pregnancy test and those parallel lines appeared. I asked if there was a history of mental health issues in her family, and she shared that her maternal side is dotted with depression, anxiety, and an aunt who was recently diagnosed with bipolar I. Keiko had struggled with anxiety symptoms since her twenties, manifesting in a variety of ways socially: in intimate relationships and in her career trajectory. This was also Keiko's first pregnancy.

Throughout her life, Keiko had been apprehensive about becoming a mother. She spoke of her fears of being "overbearing," "underloving," "perfectionistic," and "hyper-critical" in motherhood, and hence, wasn't sure she wanted to enter the maternal arena at all. She didn't expect she'd have an easy go of getting pregnant once she decided she was open to it. So when she became pregnant quickly, she found herself all the more inundated by worry about how she'd fare as a mother. During our time together, we traversed childhood issues, examined familial bonds, and unpacked relationship concerns. We explored her equivocations—their roots—and what she imagined the maternal role might entail. We were making progress.

When Keiko went in for a routine visit at the start of her second trimester, there was no heartbeat. Her devastation was far-reaching and she soon found herself engulfed by previously unexperienced levels of anxiety. Cloaked in a cocoon of sadness, Keiko upped her sessions with me. We began meeting twice a week.

Keiko focused on her physicality. "There's so much confusion going on in my body," she shared. "I mean, about my body. Well, both, I guess . . ."

Understandably, Keiko found it hard to pinpoint the words to capture this particular grief. This full-body shift. This one-day-pregnant, the-next-day-not transition. This instant transition from pregnant to not pregnant without the grueling-yet-often-rewarding hours of labor, and a newborn, to show for it.

"Yes, there is so much change going on in the body during pregnancy and when it's lost. Tell me more about yours," I said, hoping to encourage further exploration.

"I see changes I don't want to see. I feel changes I don't want to feel. How can I miss a baby I didn't even know and barely thought I wanted?"

As Keiko's size morphed from being on the precipice of robust to a postpregnancy state, she scrambled to maintain a semblance of the past. Her guilt had internalized, folding in on itself with reckless abandon, and in an effort to maintain what she thought made her a "good woman," she yearned to appear pregnant, even though she no longer was.

"I'm embarrassed to admit this, but I've been trying to keep the weight on. I've been eating my feelings. I've eaten nothing but carbs since the D&C. In search of comfort, I guess, and maybe to help pad the anxiety. I want to hold on to that puffy belly. I want to keep it close. I don't want to see it go," she shared.

"You want to be pregnant still," I said, with great understanding.

"I really, really do! I ask my boyfriend to rub my belly every night, still. I find it soothing. It makes me feel like something is still growing in there, like he's nurturing it."

In our next session, Keiko shared body-image concerns she'd navigated in her teenage years and how pregnancy— and the loss of it—stirred these visceral memories. She thought she'd "made peace with the past" but found that her miscarriage reignited ancient, loaded feelings, setting off even more anxiety.

"I grew up being compared to my sisters," Keiko shared. "I was usually the one who came up short. I wasn't as pretty, or as good in school, or as comfortable in my skin. Or at least that's what my mother always used to say. The thing is: being pregnant made me feel so beautiful and womanly, so purposeful. The change in my shape made me feel more confident. It's weird because I didn't even think I wanted to be pregnant, but now I realize how much I took to it. I'd look in the mirror and feel proud—things were changing, and it was all me."

• • •

She's right, of course. It *was* all her. The blossoming. And then the receding. It's all us. Keiko's point eloquently underscores why it can be so challenging to accept that we are fully at our bodies' mercy during pregnancy and its subsequent loss.

At twenty-seven-weeks pregnant, Hannah, an Instagram community member, messaged me after I put out a call on the @IHadaMiscarriage account saying that I'd like to talk to people about their feelings toward their bodies following pregnancy loss for an article I was writing. (I occasionally put out calls like this when I am working on a piece.) She had received news that her baby had a rare congenital condition. Her baby wouldn't make it to full term. After seeking advice from specialist after specialist, she settled on termination.

Her body had bloomed while pregnant—and still now, no longer pregnant, comments rushed in about its shape and size, including a coworker who carelessly asked when her baby was due. Salt in wounds. We want to still be pregnant, but we're not. So how do we make sense of and live on in our nonpregnant bodies, bodies that may still *feel* or continue to *look* pregnant?

Hannah reflected on her body in the wake of her termination. "Now I just feel like I look gross," she shared, defeated. "This now-empty body—with nothing to show for it, except for these newly etched-in stretch marks, a misshapen, deflating baby bump, and dripping boobs—has got to be some sort of cruel joke. And the fact that everyone thinks I'm pregnant. And the fact that I should be. I *hate* my body for this. It's all so twisted, my whole situation. All of it."

"It really is one of the worst feelings," I wrote back. Because I empathized. "To be in a body that expanded with purpose, and then is no longer pregnant. It all feels so purposeless."

. . .

Another patient, Grace, had a history of disordered eating that played a large part in the shame, guilt, and self-hate she felt following her first trimester miscarriage. In her teens, she developed both anorexia and bulimia. After years of keeping it a secret, she eventually confided in her mother, telling her she was forcing herself to purge what little food she would consume. But instead of comfort and support, her mother dismissed Grace's concerns, telling her she did not have a problem.

"She told me it was a 'white girl's disease,'" Grace explained. "And because we're Black, there was simply no way I could have had any issues surrounding food, let alone issues that might have required treatment."

While eating disorders are often billed as a "young white woman's problem," like many mental health issues, Black women are actually more likely to develop eating disorders. But a lack of access to mental health services and the trope of the "strong Black woman" make it that much more difficult for those suffering from mental health conditions like disordered eating to seek and receive treatment.[20]

From there, Grace's disordered eating proliferated unchecked. For fifteen years, she starved herself, binged, purged, and then, she told me, she would enter into imperfect recovery for a few months, sometimes a year or two, then relapse and begin the cycle once more. After repeating this pattern a few times, she became open about her eating disorder, finding comfort in friends, coworkers, and love interests; the same comfort her mother could not give her as a young adult.

Grace found out she was pregnant when she was five weeks along, and by week seven her nausea was so intense that her only respite came through consuming poppy-seed bagels, buttery pasta, and salty potato chips around the clock. Invariably, she began gaining weight, and the feeling of not having control over her body only deepened her longstanding inability to trust it. She wrestled with the inescapability of watching her body slowly but steadily grow, knowing she wanted the result of the pregnancy but loathing the physical and psychological process it takes to get there. As her discomfort grew, suddenly, at thirteen weeks along, she lost the pregnancy. And in the wake of her miscarriage, all her previous openness about her struggles with food came back to haunt her, as colleagues and friends voiced concerns about whether her history of low weight and disordered eating had caused her to miscarry.

This is, of course, *extremely* unlikely. But that doesn't change the fact that pregnancy can provoke myriad feelings for those with disordered eating habits, and may contribute to and expand upon complicated feelings about body size, shape, and self-worth that existed long before a pregnancy test showed a positive result. Eating disorders are often caused by a deep desire to maintain a semblance of ownership over one's life. And what is pregnancy if not an utter lack of control? We are at the mercy of our bodies and our hormones. Weight gain, an impending life change that can feel insurmountable, and frequent comments on a pregnant person's size all work against those who struggle with disordered eating. Grace, and others like her, find themselves ill-equipped to adequately deal with the loss of bodily autonomy that comes with pregnancy and an eating disorder's need to maintain it.

There were other factors working against Grace too. Her mother's comment—that disordered eating was a white woman's problem—continued to come up in our sessions as she waded through the guilt she felt for having miscarried. "You're stronger than this" was the underlying message. "You don't have the luxury of having these kinds of problems."

In my office, Grace was compelled to navigate the painful ramifications of the idea that her problems were miniscule at best. Her eating disorders weren't real enough for her mother to take seriously, and she had people around her suggesting that it may have even ended her pregnancy. She spoke at length about her feelings that her miscarriage was her fault, and any grief she felt as a result was superficial and self-imposed. As she parsed these emotions, we also discussed the fact that she was at the mercy of conflicting societal expectations: maintaining a certain body shape, but being "strong" enough to rise above unhealthy beauty standards or be negatively impacted by them, *and* being able to relinquish a long-held way of relating to food, control, and her body in service of a pregnancy.

Like so many of us—some far more than others—she felt as though she had been imprisoned by her body: what is expected of it, how people view it, how to maintain it, and how we are unable to completely control it.

• • •

And after a loss, we're struggling with more than just what we see when we look in the mirror. Research has found that after a miscarriage, women often report feeling a sense of alienation from their bodies. Sometimes they even report feeling "defective" and like "less of a woman."[21] Add to that the possibility of not feeling at home in your skin from hormonal changes that began when pregnancy commenced, and you're looking at one of the more challenging situations a woman can face when it comes to how she feels in her own body. For some women, this discordance is so intense that they begin feeling that their body has committed a betrayal.

Phoebe is one of those women. She responded to me on Instagram as well. She wrote that since 2016, she has had four miscarriages, and has no children.

"I used to think I was very attuned with my body. The first time I got pregnant, I felt very in touch with every little change, every tiny fluctuation," she wrote. "All my losses have happened before twelve weeks, so I've never had the opportunity to celebrate that my body can make and sustain a pregnancy into the so-called safe zone. Honestly, I can't think of anything to celebrate or to even like or appreciate about my body at this point. I feel so betrayed by it. It feels like it can't possibly belong to me, or it wouldn't have strayed so far from what I want so badly," she explained. "It's like I'm a stranger in my own skin. I feel physically unrecognizable. I'm infuriated and on the brink of defeat."

And for those who do not identify as the gender they were assigned at birth, who do not ascribe to the gender binary, or who have body dysmorphia as it relates to their identity and/or sexuality, this feeling of bodily betrayal is often compounded. From being misgendered by medical professionals to the physical signs and symptoms of pregnancy warring with their gender identity, the body becomes something of a minefield.

I heard a lot about the feeling of being at war with one's body from a relatively new patient, Taylor, who identifies as gender nonbinary. As a trans person, they do not identify with the gender they were assigned at birth. How their body has functioned throughout their life—be it the onset of puberty, menstruation, and the development of breasts—has felt like an affront to their true identity, a seemingly cruel reminder that who they are does not align with how they present. However, Taylor was pursuing artificial insemination because they believed experiencing pregnancy could be a chance to revel in the ways in which their body was made—capable of housing a baby—and perhaps even feel more connected to a form that, for them, oftentimes felt alien. With a history of body insecurity, self-esteem concerns, and percolating questions about what raising a child might look like, Taylor thought it wise to seek therapy before embarking on the journey to becoming a parent.

Taylor spoke of their theoretical future pregnancy in powerful terms, imagining that carrying a child would correlate with finally feeling "ownership" over their body, often describing the very idea of pregnancy as "primal." While Taylor told me that this attitude was often a surprise to their friends in the trans community, who sometimes find the physical act of carrying a pregnancy quite fraught with potential to fuel feelings of dysphoria, to Taylor, the thought of being pregnant offered respite from the years of body dysmorphia—obsessing over perceived "defects" or "flaws" in the body—and gender dysmorphia—the conflict between biological sex and gender identity—that had plagued Taylor since they could remember.

Taylor had considered pregnancy to be a chance at truly appreciating the profound ways in which their body was constructed—reproductive parts and all. They speculated that pregnancy could perhaps provide a transformative opportunity to look beyond the ways in which they felt betrayed by their body and, instead, get lost in its inner workings. Relish it, even. In preparing for pregnancy, Taylor had become engrossed by the mechanics of it all. After a lifetime of being unable to accept themselves physically, Taylor was beginning to get curious about and integrate the profound ways in which their body could potentially create life. And all the ways it could go wrong too.

Taylor lamented about pregnancy loss, before having experienced pregnancy at all. They opined that the possibility of miscarriage would no doubt transport them right back into childhood self-hate which centered around loathing their body. Quite literally hating the skin they were in.

"It will work, right? I'll be able to get pregnant, don't you think?" Taylor asked me, tentatively hopeful. Leading up to their scheduled intrauterine insemination procedure, we spent several sessions discussing Taylor's deep desire to experience pregnancy and the fears shrouding that aspiration. Hours before actually attempting to get pregnant, Taylor came face-to-face with debilitating panic in my office.

"What if it doesn't work?" they queried with desperation. "What if the science I've been putting so much faith in doesn't yield what I want it to?" Taylor's body lowered on the brown leather couch as they picked at tiny feathers poking out of the embroidered pillows.

We remained in silence together ever so briefly.

Witnessing their hope juxtaposed with anticipated "failure" reminded me of so many people who have sat in that exact spot—literally and figuratively—plagued by worry and sometimes optimism, imagining the worst while hoping for the best.

"I wish I knew the answer. I sincerely wish I could tell you what will happen," I said, as I thought to myself how game-changing it would be if I could somehow ensure a dreamed-of future for my patients. But I'm not a fortune teller. I can't know. I don't know. Nor am I really sure that anyone can.

Suspended in sheer vulnerability—wanting something so badly but not having a semblance of control, nothing to ensure it will come to pass—is the place of humanity. These are the heart-opening moments we wish we could evade, but can't.

"Though I can't predict the future, I hold so much hope that it'll happen for you. I know how much you want this. I understand how meaningful this is to you. You are ready to become a parent," I said.

Taylor clutched the pillows on the couch once again, looking for any additional loose, pokey feathers to extract.

I waited. And then I watched as Taylor's body crumpled in what looked like resignation. I couldn't help but wonder if they'd quickly ventured into a dark and muddled place—prematurely concluding that pregnancy wouldn't be something that could come easy.

"Are you okay?" I asked, concerned their headspace was descending.

"I don't think so." Taylor's words barely made their way

out of their lips. "I can't absorb another disappointment. I need this to happen without drama."

I understood, as I'd heard this sentiment vocalized so many times. It was then that I urged myself to gently press them to consider the possibility of this process going smoothly. For sometimes it does. So far, there was no proof it wouldn't.

"Why do you think it might not happen? What information do we have that indicates pregnancy won't happen the way you hope it will?" I wasn't attempting to shift or erase their feelings, but instead expand on them. Reveal nuance. When someone's go-to mantra is "I fail," I gingerly work to interject other possible options and outcomes.

Taylor sat quietly, mulling things over. "I don't know," they eventually said, defeat rising in their voice. "My body has let me down so many times. It's like my body and mind fail to sync up, and I want more than anything for this to be different. I deserve to have something come easily. I deserve to have an experience so many people do."

As Taylor awaited news about the outcome of their IUI, we continued on in our discussions about their fear of "failure," "not being good enough," and bubbling "self-hate." Interspersed with moments of forecasting what parenthood might look like, Taylor was pretty unequivocal about things not working out.

The following day I received a voicemail first thing in the morning. "Hi Dr. Zucker. It's Taylor. I'm not pregnant. I knew it. I knew this wouldn't happen easily for me. My body doesn't work. Any chance I can come see you today?"

Click.

This disappointing outcome is a loss of another sort. The

loss of potential. The loss of control. The loss of plans. This loss—the loss of what could have been—is yet another type of reproductive loss that American culture is not adept at speaking about with candor, nuance, or compassion.

I worried about the ways in which Taylor might use this opportunity to flagrantly heave harsh comments at themselves, further driving home the historical narrative that was already so firmly embedded. "My body fails": the refrain.

Though Taylor's exact experience is not necessarily common, their line of thinking absolutely is. After any kind of loss, or multiple losses, it's completely understandable how one could go from seeing their body as working the way it "should" to being downright traitorous. The body and failure become conflated, and as a result, a sense of alienation ensues. It's a complicated coupling.

But these bodies are our homes—whether we like it or not—and they are the only ones we have. I choose to believe my body works, that my miscarriage in no way was evidence that it doesn't. In fact, my body proved it was working the way it should be by releasing what it did. My body housed my babies, including the one I did not have the chance to know. It has labored to bring children into the world, and it has weathered the storm of a sixteen-week loss. My body also went on to become a home to my rainbow baby. If we say our bodies have failed us, we leave out all the wisdom, all the health, the transformation.

Whenever I hear about feelings of bodily alienation, failure, or body-image struggles pre- and post–pregnancy loss from patients, I listen for historical information or clues from the past that might better help me understand what's informing their current impressions. I know culture is complicit here, too, of course. And I am also keenly aware that explaining to a bereaved patient that they mustn't hate their bodies, or breaking down the very science of conception to prove these losses are no one's fault, is futile. Feelings aren't facts, and so I go where they are, while holding the hope that these feelings will evolve compassionately in time and with effort. I also know that urging someone to feel positively about their body when they simply don't can be harmful. The pressure to embody something that is not authentic—like forcing body positivity—can impede the healing process. If and when people feel like they can't disclose negative feelings, be it about their bodies or anything else, those feelings are left to fester.

We can't control how our bodies will respond to a pregnancy, nor can we dictate how they will react to a loss. All we can do is try to treat them with compassion.

## 8

*"Why did it feel as though this loss had
only happened to me?"*

"So, what are your plans for today?" Jason asked as he hap-hazardly shoved a sesame bagel toppling with lox into his mouth before taking off for work.

The nonchalant way in which he spoke stung to the core; it had been all of six days since losing the pregnancy, and I couldn't quite understand how he was able to wake up fresh-faced each day and approach the ensuing twenty-four hours with such relative ease and familiarity. As if nothing had happened. As if I hadn't been fundamentally changed.

"Not sure. Bleeding, I guess," I replied insipidly.

Of course, I probably had a laundry list of things I needed to get done—"plans" for my day that I have no doubt my husband would have much rather discussed than the blood still being collected between my legs. But each of those daily tasks felt more insignificant than the one before it. Grief's disbelief hovered full-time, and that alone was enough to manage. I was visibly defeated.

"What can I do to make this better—or at least

easier—for you?" Jason asked as he moved toward me, his eager words rich with care and concern.

I was grateful for this moment of recognition. Of connection.

He seemed so himself, so *normal*. It didn't seem possible. It didn't seem to make sense—not to me, anyway. It certainly didn't seem fair. There I was, entangled in this wretched grief, all my usual energy oozed from my worn and weeping body, and Jason's demeanor was so seemingly unaffected. I desperately longed for the partner I knew Jason to be—loving, connected, there. And perhaps selfishly, I wanted him to ache as I was aching—to feel as if I was not alone in my despair but had a partner who could feel, to some extent, the physical ramifications of a pregnancy lost, of a trauma endured. I needed us, now more than ever, in these newfound depths of mourning.

So why did it feel as though this loss had only happened to me? It didn't, of course, it happened to *us*. Together, we had a vision for our imagined family of four; a vision now marred. We had an "ours." And then we didn't. I wanted to climb into his arms and sob for hours—days, even—to nestle in and breathe together, but instead I found myself adrift, feeling like Jason was elsewhere—there but not *there*.

Between loved ones, I felt such a confounding sense of isolation. A feeling so searing, no one should know it. A feeling that should be rendered obsolete.

Jason, for his part, meant well, of course; I sensed his attentiveness, and I could see the concern in his soft, blue eyes as he intentionally focused on me for the first time all morning. I knew he wanted to help, but I was too lost in myself to help *him* help *me*. I didn't have it to give. Perhaps some semblance of tenderness or vulnerability on my part could've bridged the unforeseeable growing gap between us, but my evolving resentment and head-to-toe exhaustion shut me down. Like a clam, I slowly folded into myself.

A part of me wanted to school him on the myriad ways I'd been irreparably transformed—to plead with him about the fact that there was absolutely nothing he could do that would make any of this better. Not yet, anyway. Didn't he feel this? He'd lost a baby, too, after all. And, like me, he had seen the tiny body. So why did he appear so composed and unaffected? It was all I could do to keep from bawling. It scared me to feel this alone alongside him. Engulfed by my fresh trauma, fear hovered here and there, seemingly everywhere. Alone I wasn't, but alone I felt.

Against my better judgment, I started to see my husband as one of the many oblivious strangers walking around me as I bled into towels and held the remains of my baby in a bag. I was living out a nightmare in real time, while my husband seemed to simply live. He traipsed off to work like the people who bustled around me as I described my miscarriage to my sister. He had the capacity to revel in distraction and find solace in the creativity facilitated by his job, while I was left reckoning with this seemingly pregnant, yet hollow postpartum body of mine, and no newborn to show for it. Vacant, I was, of both baby and puissance. Witnessing the disparity between our situations was unnerving, and even though I knew that comparing his suffering to mine and mine to his was useless, I didn't make much of an effort to stop.

"You can't fix this," I mustered, slumped over my lukewarm coffee. "I wish you could, but this simply can't be fixed." I needed him to understand, but as much as I wanted to educate him on my current emotional status and attempt to find the words to express just how abhorrent I felt, I didn't have it in me. I was angry, but even more so, I was empty. Pulverized. Without.

Finally, though, I leaned in to my overwhelming anguish and wept. My head burrowed into Jason's comforting shoulder. His skin smelled like home, delicious and familiar and sweet. We held each other in the quiet of our kitchen.

I felt his unarticulated pain intermingling with my mounting misery as I watched him gather his belongings and head toward the door. He told me he'd text me periodically throughout the day, we said our I love yous, and then he was gone.

...

In those initial weeks, Jason and I processed our loss differently. Grief has that potential: to disorient and rip you from your usual place in the world, and fling you and your partner into separate and uncharted territories. There's no playbook for individuals amid this kind of grief and there surely isn't one for couples either. No warning. No shortcut.

I missed him profoundly. My lifetime partner, my love, my best friend.

It wasn't as though I couldn't see that he was sad; I knew he was hurting by the periodical downtrodden look in his eyes. His usual cheerful demeanor had dimmed, no doubt. But I was confused by—dare I say envious of—the way in which he was able to skate through the day seemingly unscathed.

I'd sit back and watch the way he easily moved from home to work and back again, how he cared for our sweet little Lievy, curious as to whether there were hints of his grief that I was missing. I wanted so badly to know how he felt; I wanted to see some tangible proof that we were traveling down this road together, but it seemed as though he was only ever skimming the surface of this earth-rattling pain. Or was he in fact drowning, but attempting to keep it together for us, for our son, for himself? For the sake of survival?

•••

Another common thread through miscarriage's aftermath (as though the loss itself weren't enough): people frequently report feeling a growing emotional distance in the context of their partnership. Feeling alone in grief alongside one's partner is another pain entirely. I hear about this often.

Recently, I connected with Simone, another woman who responded to a query on @IHadaMiscarriage after her third miscarriage. Simone explained that she and her wife, after having an in-depth discussion about how they would become parents, agreed that Simone would be the spouse to carry any future pregnancies. Her wife felt that experiencing a pregnancy would not align with how she felt about her gender, while Simone felt no such discordance. After fourteen months of trying to conceive, three miscarriages— including the loss of a twin pregnancy—and no children underfoot, Simone described a substantial rift developing between her and her partner, who "never" seemed to know the "right" thing to say. With this most recent loss, Simone and her wife didn't even know they were expecting until Simone miscarried. "It's so confusing. We're not mourning the idea of having a baby, but, we are," she told me.

It was only made harder by the fact that *she* couldn't find the words to describe this type of grief, let alone her wife. "She's not very articulate emotionally sometimes," she told me. "It makes me not want to talk about the losses at all. I hate hearing her spout clichés. It's infuriating."

And so in lies one particular cycle that can come about as couples navigate grief: One partner shuts down and then shuts the other out, or vice versa. The rift invariably grows. And each might feel misunderstood or alone, even in the presence of the other.

Other times, however, it is the partner who instigates conversations about loss, and pines to connect in grief. This is the case with Maeve, an Instagram connection I made some years ago—after her first of two stillbirths and a miscarriage. I've talked to Maeve occasionally, through the highs and lows in her marriage. Initially plunging headfirst into the depths of despair after her first stillbirth, Maeve just as soon popped out of it. She wanted nothing to do with the topic, and told her husband as much.

"Talking about grief isn't helping it go away. I just don't want to talk about it anymore, but it seems it's all he ever wants to do," she shared with me. Maeve wanted to "go back to the life they had before" and shuddered whenever her husband spoke of their babies, gone. Though she remains sad, her hushed mourning process feels more comfortable to her than speaking aloud about all of the emotions that arise on any given day. "I honor my babies in my own way. Quietly," she wrote, and expressed a hope that her husband would do the same. "There's a part of me that just wants to pretend like none of this ever happened. I'm tired of being tired. I'm tired of talking." Fed up with grief, Maeve longed for respite. A hiatus from it all. Yet another prevailing feeling I hear about throughout my days: a desire for grief's reprieve.

For Raven, the grief of her pregnancy losses hearkens back to the untimely death of her mother. Her mom died suddenly just after Raven's twenty-first birthday, and the pain of this significant loss remains palpable, resurfacing most poignantly upon receiving the news of her missed miscarriage. Raven shared with me about her complicated ectopic pregnancy and her missed miscarriage over direct message on Instagram, when I was working on a piece about relationships. She and her boyfriend met soon after her mother's death, and his not having known her mother seems to compound the pain of each successive pregnancy loss.

Raven described her relationship with her boyfriend as loving and effusive. They talked openly about their respective fears, which her pregnancy losses had cemented. She worried, though, that if these pregnancy losses continued and they couldn't have a baby together, somehow the relationship wouldn't last. She hid this worry from him, and told me that this is the first time she's ever not been direct with him about issues in the relationship. Raven's careening feelings took her out of the present and into her head more often than not.

"I don't blame myself but I also do, and I wonder if he does too. He says we're in this for the long haul, but what if these losses undo us?" Raven said. "What if the love fades? I want him to be with someone who can have children. If I can't, I feel like I don't deserve him."

There are myriad ways grief affects couples, and we see here some universal themes as well as some very specific examples of how loss impacts coupledom, communication, identity, and interpersonal connection. Because loss stirs a range of individual as well as collective feelings—perhaps born of childhood experiences or much more recent events—and because there exists no reference book for navigating loss, we are left to break ground on our own. Together.

...

Instead of shutting down, I revved up: I became angry. It wasn't fair or justified, but I was confounded. I was torn apart, and I was equal parts jealous and frustrated that Jason seemed to be so coolly surviving a loss that had nearly snuffed me out altogether, both in body and in mind. And truthfully, my temporary vitriol felt like a welcome reprieve from the heartache that had taken center stage since my miscarriage. Whereas that deep sadness wore me down, my rage served to bolster me with supposed strength and a focused resolve.

I look back now and see quite clearly that my anger was actually a weapon of hope in the midst of what felt like a hopeless experience. The fuel that propelled me forward was only available in an active emotion like anger, and nowhere else in those fraught days following our loss. I was scared to crumble—to let the vulnerability consume me—and to be soft through it all, so I clutched onto anger, which in retrospect served as a wedge. Unproductive though it was, I was doing my best.

At hints of my glaring disappointment, Jason would work to allay the hostility radiating off of me. "We're in this together," he would say. But unfortunately, these utterances didn't penetrate. After all, were we really? I couldn't find evidence of that companionship and connection that had up until this time existed effortlessly between us. His breasts weren't swelling with milk, seemingly taunting him. He wasn't constantly changing blood-soaked pads: a visceral reminder of what my body had previously shed. He wasn't watching his body erase the physical evidence of a pregnancy that ended far too soon.

It didn't feel like we were "in this together" in those early days. Instead, I found myself wondering whether or not he was even capable of meeting me in the depths at all, since it hadn't physically happened to him. I wondered whether he was opting out of taking that deep dive in an attempt at self-preservation. Either way, it was painful. I envied that he seemed to have the choice at all.

...

Jason tried assuaging my fear by telling me we'd make it through this. "We'll have another baby," he'd say. He assured me that when we did, things would be different. But I had a tough time believing in visions of some hopeful future that lay on the horizon. The concept of having another baby was no consolation at all, really. This was apples and oranges. The conception of another baby would in no way erase the trauma of how things unfolded, and what was more, this loss was mire I had to wade through before I could even begin again.

One night about a month after the loss, after Liev had long since gone to sleep, I pulled out some ice cream from the freezer and expressed my concern and disappointment over our emotional distance, and over the way in which

Jason seemed largely unfazed by what was surely the most devastatingly formative experience of our marriage, much less our lives.

"I've felt so alone," I told him, crying. "I wish we'd been in this together more. Have you even been sad about this?" I asked, sounding at once desperate and frustrated.

He was taken aback. Understandably thrown by my query, he responded indignantly. "Of course I've been sad! But it's not like there's an instruction manual for how to navigate this!" he said, clearly baffled at my gall.

He went on: "You're making it seem like this experience didn't happen to both of us. It's not fair. We both lost this baby. We both lost what we hoped would be our larger family. A sibling for Liev. A joyous event."

Relief overtook me. I was reassured to hear grief was on his mind and that he'd been considering our lives and how they'd changed. It's not that I wanted my husband to be in emotional pain—to feel what I had been feeling. I would not wish that on anyone. But I wanted—needed—to feel as if this pregnancy and the subsequent, traumatic loss of it mattered to him as it mattered to me. I needed to know that it was as real for him as it was for me. I needed to know that my grief was valid, and could be touched and felt by someone else.

"Thank you for letting me in," I sighed with gratitude. "I've wondered where you've been. I have missed you. Us. I just wasn't sure how you've been feeling, since you haven't been talking much about it."

His point was wholly valid. He was right; I'd had an impossible time trying to grasp an understanding of his experience, because he so rarely shared it with me. I couldn't read his mind, nor could he read mine; and the ways in which our respective pain had manifested itself had quickly turned us into virtual strangers.

"I want to know how you feel," I reiterated. All the hours that I'd spent in mourning and anxiety manifested themselves in the tears that began rolling heavily down my cheeks. It might sound curious, but what a breath of fresh air this was, to be going deeper together.

The rest of that night unfolded in a long-overdue, free-flowing discussion of Jason's feelings, his experience, his perspective, and his grief. "I am sad. I've been sad. Somehow I feel hopeful, though. I feel like this won't happen again; that the next pregnancy will go smoothly."

*Lucky you*, I was tempted to say, but resisted. My resentment threatened to take hold again as I considered what a place of privilege a sentiment like that came from. He wouldn't have to be the pregnant one. He didn't have the blood-stained underwear, the tingling nipples, the altered waistline. He didn't live in the body that expelled the pregnancy; didn't feel abandoned by it, confused by it, tormented by it. He trusted things would be okay based on hope and fantasy, not facts or peering into a crystal ball.

But I withheld; I was so tired of fighting against both him and myself, and I knew I needed to relent and give him room to process safely in my presence. So I proceeded in giving him the space to explain to me the form his grief had taken in the minutes, hours, and days after he'd flown through our front door only to find me bleeding and in shock on the toilet, a dead baby on the brown hand towel a few feet away on the turquoise-tiled counter, lovely and lost.

He'd been *terrified*, I learned. He'd seen me in a pool of my own blood, shaking and hemorrhaging. He'd heard my voice, uncannily focused, as I instructed him to put our baby in a bag to bring to my doctor's office for testing. He'd watched me somehow brave the unfathomable pain during my unmedicated emergency D&C procedure. And all of it was so otherworldly, so far from anything he could've imagined, that retreating within himself was all he could do to keep from falling apart. He had been doing exactly as I had been: we had each subsisted on parallel tracks of pressing forward by any means necessary. I had been so focused on mine, I hadn't realized how similar his really was.

What he saw unfold in his mind's eye was the instantaneous unraveling of our family—his wife and baby lost (because what if I had died there in our bathroom that day?), his son motherless, and a carefully mapped-out future gone in an instant. His mind had been firing on all cylinders. "What's happening? Why us? Not us. Not us. This can't be real," he'd pleaded internally. It was a panicked, desperate narrative that played steadily on repeat in his mind. He was exhausted and afraid.

In the madness of it all, I let my own devastation become deep disdain, to the point that I hadn't seen or understood that Jason had retreated deep within himself in order to find the tools and strength he needed to process his pain and put one foot in front of the other with resolve. When Jason saw both the physical and emotional effects this miscarriage had on me, he did the only thing he could think of in order to stay afloat. He adopted the *I. Must. Survive.* narrative and kept moving.

...

Ten days after the loss, my doctor rang with the results of the pathology tests. She had thought it may take a bit longer, so her call was unexpected. I anxiously awaited her words and hoped there was something to learn, as I knew it was possible the tests wouldn't necessarily point to the reason why. Her voice had energy in it and her tone was purposeful, which gave me a smidge of hope she had news that might solve this mystery.

"A chromosomal abnormality—47 XXX or trisomy X—was identified," she reported.

Anxiety lifted almost immediately, as this information indicated there were concrete medical facts—biological reasons—elucidating why this pregnancy ended as it did.

She explained in detail what this meant. Triple X syndrome is a genetic disorder that affects approximately one in one thousand female fetuses. Females typically have two X chromosomes in all cells—one X chromosome from each partner. In triple X syndrome, however, a female has three X chromosomes.

It was unnerving and paradoxical to feel such intense relief amid this gooey, tar-like heartache I'd been stranded in. But this news gave Jason and I the data we needed to understand that this death was not without reason or rationale. It gave me the space to understand my body; it had known what I didn't, and had used that information in a way nature had intended. It made sense now, though emotionally it all still felt so nonsensical, of course. But in some very important ways, this news allowed for a welcomed shift in our thinking, particularly about our reproductive futures. In essence, this definitive news was a (re)affirmation of what I'd felt: that my body had not failed; that it was working as it should.

•••

I hung up the phone.

"Look; I know we'd both been keen on you having an unmedicated birth, but this wasn't exactly what I had in mind," Jason joked as he gently cupped my face in his hands. And at once, we were laughing, kissing, and bantering; that bridge that joined us together began to form, and I felt those old familiar feelings of intimacy and ease. I'd missed him, wanted him, and so desperately needed him; and here, at long last, was an emotional reunion. Here was my partner, my best friend, and the man who'd experienced all of this horror right alongside me, tortured at the idea of losing everything he loved in the blink of an eye.

Haggard but hopeful, we made it through together. Though our grief flung us apart for a short stint, it ultimately served as common ground. It was, after all, our only way forward. In the end, born from the loss of our daughter was an ability to exercise compassion for each other at new heights, to respect the other's humanity and deeply personal emotional experience and reaction to grief.

Through our loss, we realized exactly how much a marriage holds the ability to endure, how strong a union between two people can be, and the extent to which we can learn multitudes about ourselves and each other. We welcomed, at long last, a renewed connection and a hard-won understanding of what resilience we possess in the face of death.

# 9

*"Can pleasure and grief coexist?"*

As I've combed through the various elements of life after loss, I'm struck by the ways in which loss can upend even our very personal and often complicated relationships with our bodies. Pregnancy can leave us intimately connected with them one moment, then feeling as if we're veritable strangers the next. Or worse yet, despising or rejecting the very body we've been assigned, the one we must continue to live in.

Pregnancy loss can and often does serve as a reminder that our bodies, regardless of shape, size, color, or function, behave outside our control. Our bodies can become the key source of our discontent and grief, especially when we cannot will them to become or stay pregnant. Considering the feelings of betrayal that so often invade the minds of people who've experienced pregnancy loss, we might become prone to reassessing exactly how we feel about our bodies, how we feel in them, how we touch them, and, critically, how we like them to be touched.

We find ourselves reckoning with a coupling that is

deeply troubling in nature: the intermingling of death and desire. Even though a woman may feel adrift after a pregnancy loss, she still exists as a sexual being—but how do you balance the two? Desire might wane in the face of loss. It might increase. It might remain relatively unchanged. I would like to think we can all agree that we deserve tenderness amid grief, and that such a thing can certainly come about by way of sexual intimacy. And in many instances, expressing sexual desire can serve as a coping mechanism. So as we begin to acknowledge our ability to possess the potential to soothe and rebuild from loss, sex can act as a conduit to elemental connection. Then again, maybe not.

Maybe our genitals or bodies themselves become specifically associated with loss, making it difficult to return to pleasure, as either a form of healing or simply for the sake of it. Does this site then become a source of anxiety, comfort, fear, dread? Toss some unanticipated grief into the mix, and, *bam*! The footing you thought you had is likely no longer. Sex and intimacy present one crucial question that we must reckon with post-loss: Can pleasure and grief coexist?

Pregnancy and everything surrounding it already has the power to change sex—its meaning, its purpose, its function, its feeling. Sometimes, once couples begin trying to conceive, the mood shifts, especially if it isn't an easy road to conception (but this can also occur when conception happens fast). And because returning to sex after pregnancy loss also carries the potential of getting pregnant once again, hope and heartache might intertwine in a place previously uncomplicated by these notions. I've talked to so many women about this, because, as you can see, it is layered and intensely complex.

For some, sex stops being a bonding point or a way to

experience pleasure, and starts becoming rote, or even unpleasant. This happened to one member of my Instagram community, Yael, who messaged me when I asked for stories about this issue. "I didn't really want to have sex. We only did it to try to conceive. I used to like sex a lot—we had a really great sex life. But when we were trying to get pregnant again after the loss, it just became a task. I didn't even physically enjoy it anymore. I think my fear got in the way." This is not an uncommon reaction.

Pregnancy loss has the power to affect the way some women feel in and about their bodies, and how they want to share (and not share) them sexually.

I remember talking to Jade, one of my patients who experienced this shift in her sexual desire—and the many ways in which it impacted her relationship—after she lost a pregnancy at nine weeks along. "Some days things feel totally copacetic between us, and others it feels like we're on different planets. He's just so . . . *unchanged*," she said. "Making it through to the end of a day feels like a feat in itself, emotionally speaking. So when it comes time to go to bed, all I want to do is sleep. Not cuddle, not talk, not kiss. I just want the day to end so my grief can finally take a beat. And yet time after time, Ben will crawl in next to me and press his body against mine." She continued, "It's a loving act, I know, he just wants to reconnect physically—to bond—and . . . it's just too soon. It's the last thing on earth I want to do right now."

Later in our session, Jade articulated feeling badly about her lack of interest in returning to sexual intimacy. She worried that her lack of interest was hurting her partner somehow, but her primal need to retreat took precedence. As it sometimes must.

My patients and the people in my communities continually reflect on the fact that among the grieving, there exists a recurrent theme: for so many, sexuality shifts, increases, gets lost, or, at the very least, is mired in the weeds of reproductive complications. Its meaning changes. Desire contorts. Some divest in physical connection altogether. I've heard stories of people retreating from their partners, burying their sexuality deep beneath their grief, oftentimes feeling undeserving of or wholly disinterested in pleasure. I've also heard stories of women wanting more than their partners can provide; of new fantasies taking hold and of the desire to experience more than one sexual partner—a want often rooted in the need to feel in control of the body and the ways in which it can be used.

These potential outcomes exist partially because there are so many conflicting thoughts firing simultaneously in the mind, affecting the body. Some berate their bodies, others divorce them, some are tender and loving to them. Those who come to pregnancy loss with an already complex relationship with their bodies can find a newfound appreciation for the way their bodies work; burying themselves in the science of it all and becoming fixated on the statistics, the medicine, the intricate cogs of procreation. And others take that troubled relationship and, in the wake of a miscarriage, destroy any fragile appreciation they had for their body entirely.

This happened to Yael too. "I generally dislike my body. I'm very self-conscious, but usually my husband makes me feel really good about my body," she said. "After my loss, I hated my body all the more. Despised it. And now it wasn't about how it looked, but the fact that it *failed*. He couldn't help me with that." Her feelings spiraled. "I hated my body so much. It was hard to want to experience pleasure, because I didn't even want to look at myself, touch myself, be touched. I was so angry at my body because it wasn't doing what it was supposed to do. 'Why is this happening? What is wrong with me? What is wrong with my body?' It was a whole-new realm of body loathing that I still haven't really gotten over. These feelings trumped my negative feelings about my body image, but I constantly felt like it was failing me. And in turn, it was failing everyone I touched. I thought, 'Look at how many people my defective body is impacting. Look at how my body is causing grief for others.'"

In sessions, women wondered how they'd pick up the pieces of their now-fractured lives, including how they'd return to sex. "How can I even think about having sex right now?" This question would float around with regularity, the women asking themselves just as much as they were posing the question to me. Women who'd gone through miscarriage, stillbirth, and infant loss would come to me expressing how sex was the last thing they wanted—how their desire for intimacy had tuckered out. "I don't feel it. It's lost, and I don't even know if I want to find it again," they'd say, inadvertently turning their backs on the basic concept of sensuality. As with Yael, their sex drives may have existed healthily before their trauma—thrived, even—but post-loss, the idea of being sexual felt invasive, sometimes disloyal, scary, offensive. Entertaining the idea of personal sexual arousal, let alone pleasuring another, felt like a confusing betrayal—a lewd form of disrespect to the pressing issue at hand: their grief. This is, of course, common in many individuals in the throes of mourning a death or a loss. But the difference with pregnancy loss specifically is that the body—the sex organs—is the *physical site* of the grief. "My vagina was a constant reminder of the loss," came a response from Sasha, another member of my online community. "Because this place was a site of pain, I wasn't able to just click back over to pleasure or wanting to have sex freely."

Women in this mindset see sex—and masturbation, for that matter—as a self-indulgent act that symbolizes an erasure of their grief in favor of emotional or physical or personal gain. These feelings are, of course, compounded by societal messaging that pigeonholes women as maternal, not sexual. In a culture that already discourages women—especially moms or those who will one day become moms—to embrace and express their sexuality, how can we possibly feel free to return to our sexual selves in the midst of our grief? We are judged under the best of circumstances.

Aliyah, a member of my online community who had a stillbirth at thirty weeks, said her sex life with her partner was difficult for the next two years. But she couldn't be alone either. "Masturbation felt selfish. Something so sacred [my stillbirth] happened there, so it felt selfish to not include my husband there too. I felt alienated from my body. I had to rebuild a relationship with my body all over again."

In contrast, for some women, masturbation was the only available kind of sexual expression. Libby messaged me after her termination, which was due to life-threatening preeclampsia, and we discussed this exact reaction.

"Masturbation was the only way I could reach orgasm, actually, because I wasn't performing, it was just for myself," she said. "After my loss, it was very difficult for me. My husband had taken care of me in a new way—taking me to the bathroom, helping me out. It was so vulnerable and—not in a sexy way—very intimate. Masturbating, I didn't have to think about him or his thoughts. I could cancel out the noise of what he might be thinking or seeing after watching me lose our baby. I was too afraid to ask him what he saw. What he thought. My self-esteem was already so compromised. And I was worried that my anxieties would become his too. But I had a lack of self-consciousness when it came to masturbating. It was a step toward self-care to masturbate."

This is not to say that anyone should feel inhibited, embarrassed, or guilty if they *do* want to have sex. As Libby points out, masturbation and sex can be compassionate acts of self-care and restorative for romantic relationships. Take this message from Trina, a member of the Instagram community: "I felt like my body had failed me in losing my son three days after he was born. I'm single, but I sought out sexual partners because sex was a way to gain that back—to feel powerful in my body again. There was some guilt that came with the pleasure in the early days, but finding joy while navigating the self-facing, negative self-blame helped me navigate in a more clear-minded and balanced way. Sex helped me remember who I was."

Each time the concept of sex and sexual pleasure would come up—whether in sessions with my patients where I could sit and discuss it with them, or through a direct message on Instagram—I'd encourage those who shared to trust their feelings, to honor their instincts, and to abide by the schedule that felt right. It was rarely straightforward, of course. Some were afraid sex might lead to another loss, which oftentimes led to feelings of guilt that arose over abstaining from intimacy with their partners. Then guilt would compound further, as they found themselves swirled up inside a narrative that was wholly destructive: Stricken by the loss of a future they'd envisioned and immobilized by the bone-shattering grief that ensued, they believed that they were somehow to blame for what had happened. That these unthinkable circumstances had come about as a result of something they'd done. Or not done. That their bodies had failed. If they couldn't trust their bodies to carry out the very thing they were purportedly designed to do, they reasoned, why should they allow themselves to feel pleasure?

The return of joy can take time, of course. Pleasure and grief, after all, might never have been considered mutually exclusive if not for the harmful cultural stigmatization surrounding pregnancy loss. Tapping back into our sexuality is certainly not the only way to reconnect with our deeper selves and regain confidence in our sensuality, but it undoubtedly holds the power to offer the comfort and encourage the connection that our minds and bodies so often crave.

Amelia confided in me via direct message that she cried the first time she had sex with her husband after her pregnancy loss. "It was about six weeks later, when we returned to penetrative sex. I cried right after because I finally felt really *connected* to my husband again. With my loss, I felt like I was on an island—water between me and everybody. When we had sex, I cried with relief to be connected to someone again. Because of that, I think that pleasure and grief must coexist."

Surveying the emotional damage that can occur after a loss and realizing the extent of mental labor that must go into processing it, these women would oftentimes shelve sexual engagement until they could find their footing. And understandably so. Sensuality took on new meaning. And pregnancy too. So, no matter where a woman was in her grief process, my advice to her during our sessions would remain unchanged: "If you don't want to have sex," I would tell them, "then don't. If you do, then you should." And of course, this advice applied to nonpatients too. It certainly applied to me.

• • •

A month after my miscarriage, I returned to my obstetrician's office for a follow-up appointment. She took a look at my uterus and cervix to be sure they looked normal, and we discussed whether Jason and I wanted to try again. Her recommendation was to wait three cycles before trying to conceive—if we decided to—and she otherwise checked in on my emotional state.

I felt a dozen emotions all in synchronicity when I got that first period following pregnancy loss. The blood: its color, its meaning. A flood of grief. That at-least-your-body-is-working mantra. Remembering the blood that indicated the beginning of the end. A glaring reminder that I was no longer pregnant. Starting again, maybe. Anticipation. Hope that there will be future pregnancies that last. Not knowing. No control. A surreal state of being. Loss of an identity you once knew and thought of as ironclad. Menstruation can mean so many different things to women around the globe, and for those of us who have miscarried, that first period post-loss can trigger unimaginable memories . . . and maybe even a little bit of hope.

That hope hurled me back into that space—the physical act of potentially getting pregnant again, the mental strength that must accompany a post-loss pregnancy, and the emotional toll that the magnitude of such a thing would take on my ailing mind. I was still reeling from the trauma I'd just lived through, but tucked in somewhere deep was a trust that this would not happen again. It just couldn't. And so, we proceeded.

I could choose to wait out the months or years it might take to emotionally recover, or I could choose to try to conceive again. I couldn't have both. I was forty by then, and Jason had just turned forty-one, so we were well aware time wasn't something we had to waste. And so I (re)embraced my recently established desire for a larger family and went through the motions, because on some level, I knew I wanted to. I wanted to, even though I also *didn't* want to. The fear of getting pregnant again was just as intimidating as *not* being able to get pregnant again.

And it was there that I found myself once again immersed in another aspect of a struggle I'd heard time and again, from patients within the confines of my office and online among other loss moms. Countless women had recounted to me their fears of sexual engagement, of conceiving again, of *not* conceiving again, reckoning with their altered sexual identities and sometimes suppressing their own desires altogether. And here I was, again able to empathize in a way that was only possible after experiencing such a thing firsthand.

# 10

*"We are not going down on this note."*

"My friend Jasmine keeps pressing me—she won't stop asking if I've started thinking about trying again," Ella told me. She sat across from me, legs and arms crossed, head leaning on the back of the firm, brown leather couch. She plucked a Kleenex from the nearby box. "It's just weird that something so private—so individual—is asked so nonchalantly. Like somehow my sex life is a public matter now," she said, on edge. It was uncanny to be having this conversation with her, when people had been asking me the very same thing.

"You felt pressured to share something you weren't quite ready to talk about," I remarked.

"Yeah, it was awkward. But I told her that I had," she replied. "I didn't tell her that we're already trying, though. I just said something about how we'll get to it when the time feels right." Ella continued, "She has two kids, and has some fairy-tale story—like, she got pregnant with both on the first try or something. No miscarriages, no pregnancy fears, no nausea, even, so she just doesn't get it. I don't know . . . I just wasn't in the mood to talk about it with her. Wrong audience, or something—you know?"

"I understand," I said. "And trying again—how do you feel about the prospect of that? Are you feeling ready?"

"You know, I really do, actually," Ella replied. "I finally got my period, and I'm just so ready to get back into a good place again. Less bogged down. I'm tired of feeling like my loss is what defines me. I just want to be pregnant again."

"That makes sense. Feeling reduced to a loss is not a good feeling. You are more than your loss. So much more, of course," I empathized.

"Thank you. I think so. My life is about so much more than grief. It's got to be. And I think being pregnant again will bring some much-needed hope to our household. I'm curious, though, how easy it'll be this time around. Or how hard. I'm in this private women's group on Facebook, and I asked how long it took each of them to get pregnant again after they'd miscarried."

"What were the responses like?" I asked, admittedly at least partially curious for personal reasons.

"They were varied, but most people got pregnant again within a few cycles, give or take. One woman said it took her nine months. This frightened me to no end. It had better *not* take me that long. I don't think I could handle that: The ongoing, unrelenting disappointment. The reiteration of loss through negative pregnancy tests. That grief. Getting my period again and again would feel like loss after loss, I think."

"I can understand why hearing that would spike your fear," I said. "It can be tempting to compare time frames, but everyone's situation is unique, and it can sometimes hurt more than help when we survey what other people have gone through."

Silently, I hoped that it wouldn't take long for Ella, and by proxy, myself. I also considered how challenging it can be to not have access to answers. To simply not know. And while Ella never asked me how long I imagined she would have to try before getting pregnant again, so many women do. "Do you think I'll get pregnant again?" they'll ask in angst, and it takes everything in me not to automatically respond with a guarantee about a future I cannot adequately predict. I want this for these women if and when they want it for themselves. And because hope is vital, I hold it almost always, at least for those who need it. And because uncertainty is such a tough place to live— within our psyches, and within our bodies—I want to shout yes from rooftops: *you will get pregnant again.* But I don't know. I just know that not everyone does get pregnant and so I mustn't say a thing. I resist the reflex to enthusiastically say yes, as I know not what the future holds.

· · ·

I understand this too well: The yearning to bypass trial and error. To just know—to find out somehow—what will come next, with some degree of definiteness. No one, of course, could predict if I'd get pregnant again, but I will admit, I searched high and low for answers. In those desperate moments of disquieting uncertainty, I turned to places I never thought I'd go. Grasping to glean insight, I turned to, of all places, a psychic. Vivian.

Vivian's office was just south of Santa Monica Boulevard, on the west side of the street on Camden Drive in the heart of Beverly Hills. Since her office was only about a twenty-minute walk from my own, I arrived early and apprehensive. I'd never done this before—search for

Vivian greeted me with the air of someone regal as I glanced around her space to get a sense of her. A mix of faux flowers in dusty glass vases, stuffed animals, and several photographs of famous people in Lucite frames sat on the paint-chipped windowsill. *Did these people really come here?* We sat down around a thick walnut, oval table and she began shuffling cards. "Tell me when to stop," she said. "Okay . . . Stop." I was just playing along. I didn't have a clue what we were doing.

She flipped the card over. "Do you have a son?"

"I do."

Then, more shuffling. "Stop!" I exclaimed again. I was getting the hang of this now.

Vivian flipped another. "And you have a daughter?"

I hesitated. I was there for answers—not hide-and-seek—so rather than wait to see if she could guess what I'd just been through, I decided to share. "Maybe you're picking up on my recent loss. I had a miscarriage, in the second trimester. It was a girl."

There was a pause. A pregnant pause.

"No, no. No, that's not it. You will have a daughter," she said without hesitation.

"Really?" I said, perhaps a bit too skeptically.

I found her confidence fascinating, if not a little troubling.

"Why would I tell you that you were going to have a healthy daughter if you weren't? This wouldn't benefit you or me to tell you this if it wasn't true," she announced, her voice at once haughty and benevolent.

She had a point.

"And this girl has your eyes almost exactly, darling. Green and open wide, taking in the world with poise, just like you."

Silence sat between us as I ventured to digest the enormity of what she'd said with aplomb. And then it dawned on me that this interchange could surely get my hopes up (high, *way* too high) and how much more dashed they'd be if she was wrong. *What if this is all just make-believe? And what if she'd said I wouldn't get pregnant again? Would this affect my next move?*

We held eye contact.

She continued, "Sometimes things happen to us and they deepen our work. They incite a metamorphosis or a deepening of something we've already started. I believe your loss will do this."

She hadn't been privy to my last name, so there was no chance she'd googled me prior to my appointment; it seemed eerie that perhaps she was alluding to my practice and specialty. "What do you mean?" I asked.

"This loss of yours will help you affect others that have gone through similar experiences—this could be through service or writing or public speaking or other avenues, but whatever it is, your impact is needed."

She was way off on other things she covered in our time together, but the things that were spot-on left me chilled for days. She was so sure. How could she be *so* sure?

Nevertheless, Vivian's assuredness came and left my weary psyche almost as quickly as it'd blazed in—and I was right back where I'd started. *Will I get pregnant quickly again? Have another loss? Or might I not even get pregnant at all?* Her certainty hadn't fully assuaged my concerns, so I was back to square one. No amount of crystal balls, shuffled stacks of tarot cards, or sorcery could convince me. I'd have to brave pregnancy again if I wanted to find out for sure.

•••

*Are you going to try again?* The question itself seems innocent enough—albeit incredibly personal—but considering it after experiencing pregnancy loss can be cumbersome. The question looms. It often comes from others around us—those closest to us, gently or not-so-gently prodding to see if we're feeling ready to make another attempt, and those on the outside of our circles who are less informed, reminding us offhandedly that our older child(ren) seems ready for a sibling or that it's "about time" we have a child. But it's not always like this—sometimes we find it percolating primarily within ourselves. And though it seems like a simple question, the answer is not necessarily altogether straightforward. After all, a loss holds the power to alter the way someone feels about pregnancy for good. Not always, of course, but sometimes. With loss can come a greater awareness of vulnerability—mortality even—now knowing too well what it feels like to lose something once growing inside of us. If we choose to dive in again, how do we relinquish the control that we never had to begin with, but somehow thought we did? Will this newfound awareness of our lack of control haunt us as we consider trying again, and perhaps accompany us through the next pregnancy, if there is one? How will it feel to try? What if we don't get pregnant? What if we *do*?

I've seen a wide gamut of reactions from women in my office as they consider this complicated next step. Some are paralyzed in their grief and, as I've mentioned, unable to contemplate sex, let alone think about another pregnancy—not yet, anyway. Some, as I've also described, are crippled by an erroneous fear that there is something wrong with their bodies in general or their wombs more specifically, and that loss will invariably happen again if/when they become pregnant. Some might become, as Ella seemed to be, fueled by an unconscious competitive drive or a game of comparing and contrasting. They unknowingly take stock of the women in their lives—who's lost a pregnancy and who hasn't, who's gotten pregnant quickly and who hasn't—and make some sort of unwitting goal to beat their competition in order to prove to themselves that they can. All these different reactions are common and normal amid the transition—especially when there is such a profound mismatch between what we want and what we sometimes do or do not receive.

● ● ●

Within the confines of our own home, the topic of expanding our family was one my husband and I didn't truly contemplate until Liev was over three years old. I wanted to take things one step at a time: Start with one child and go from there. See how it felt. Parent for a while. Discover who Liev was and who I would be as a mother. And then, from there, decide what we wanted for our family.

When I was pregnant for the first time, it thrilled me to think about how both Jason and I would rise to the task of becoming parents, and how we'd undertake this as a team. *What a playful and inspiring parent he will be*, I'd think, *and I, the practical and grounding force*. We'd do this well together, I trusted, and could hardly wait to see a cooing baby in my husband's loving embrace, and the eventuality of him coaching some sort of sport eight years down the road. Jason's vision for our family was similar, except he has a twin and as such, he saw great value in our son having a sibling—and us as a couple being at the helm of a larger clan. For him, this was sort of automatic. For me, it was a process. He and his brother are so close—they work together, they consult with each other on decisions big and small, and they harbor a connection that's both inherent and a result of intentional effort. Jason saw nothing but boundless benefits to being a sibling and therefore having one for Liev, and for us as parents too.

•••

Getting pregnant with my son was easy. The subsequent months of his development were filled with surprising enjoyment, international travel, and wild anticipation of who this little person would be and what the journey of motherhood would feel like. I adored pregnancy—I relished my growing bump, the fetal hiccups, napping constantly, and daydreaming about the unknown.

As the years pressed on, I marveled both at how complicated mothering could be and how simple it was to love him beyond definition.

Soon, I became an avid proponent of having "only one" child. *Why steal attention and focus from him by juggling two?* I thought I was onto something novel, as if I had just realized I had a choice in the matter. I wondered, if I had more than one, whether I might invariably meld into an overwhelmed soup of mismatched ingredients by adding another personality to the mix. *Why would anyone opt for that?* I thought to myself on numerous occasions while glancing at harried moms with two children fervently running in opposite directions at the park. "One and done," I enthusiastically declared whenever questioned about whether or not I'd be joining the multiple-children set. I spoke with a certain sort of pride and commanding resoluteness about focusing on my son, my work, and some version of a balanced existence between those.

And then I changed my mind. Or, perhaps more accurately, because my husband had envisaged raising two children, it was time for me to think through, in a more serious and nuanced way, what he wanted. What we wanted. What we felt we could handle. I took some months to marinate on the idea of growing our family in the context of my age and our imagined future. I wanted to excavate my decision-making a bit more, to delve a little deeper into what it might be like to rethink the family arrangement. Could I recalibrate the picture I had so firmly become used to in my mind of our thriving family of three? Would I have the emotional stamina to raise another human being? And if so, who might this person be, and who would the three of us become as a result of this change in dynamic?

I came to realize that for me, having a second child somehow signified committing to adulthood even more so than I already had. Not that I fancied myself a perpetual kid by any means, but somehow, I was resisting—staving off—the next phase of my development by foreclosing on the idea of engaging in motherhood a second time around. It meant growing up a little more, I thought, and I wasn't sure I wanted to do that. So I urged myself to look into previously unexplored places in my psyche to get a handle on where these thoughts were coming from, who I was, and who I wanted to be, maternally and more generally. There was a lot to consider. This identity conundrum required me to deliberate long and hard.

I ultimately decided that I wanted to find out.

Almost as quickly as the first time around, I found myself holding a welcomed positive pregnancy test. Unlike my pregnancy with Liev, however, my head was tucked in the toilet bowl morning, noon, and night. Sick as a dog, I dragged myself around, hoping the second trimester would grace me with less ghastly symptoms and some much-needed peace. But those late-morning drops of blood that appeared in the bathroom of my dermatologist's office at sixteen weeks along signaled that calm wasn't coming. A relationship that had barely begun was no longer. My four-month-long pregnancy was done. I had been so pleased by how swiftly this new pregnancy had arrived, yet devastated by how hastily it had left. How strange, the ways in which the passing of time can be both a comfort and a torment.

The end of my daughter's short existence spurred on the beginning of my altered, grieving life. So much had changed—and I soon realized how earnestly and readily my soul had begun preparing for another child. Even if I could have gone back in time, I flirted, would I?

...

There were many reasons that it wasn't long before the *will I try again?* question started looping on high speed in my mind after our loss. It was daily, in fact, that I found myself turning the idea around in my head—and depending on my frame of mind, it was either something that would ignite me or scare me outright. While there was a version of me who wanted nothing to do with being pregnant again, there also existed another part of me that saw a subsequent pregnancy as an opportunity to reset, to rebuild, and to perhaps create the larger family we both now wanted.

*We are not going to go down on this note* was a mantra my

husband and I quipped about, one that playfully got us to put one foot in front of the other even when our collective grief was blinding. Luckily, moments of humor and optimism showed themselves, despite how bogged down we got. We could rely on each other for laughs and a pinch of positivity amid those ambiguous days.

So it was decided: we were going to try again. We wanted to. We wanted to make every effort to *not go down on this note*. And so, we dared to undertake pregnancy once more. Was this courage, stupidity, denial, ego? I guess I'll never know exactly, but I think it was a little bit of each.

And just like that, there they were: those two familiar pink lines. A positive pregnancy test. Again. Jason and I were equal parts relieved and petrified. As consoling as it was to be pregnant once more, I carried with me the heavy weight of possibility. Knowing well that what happened to me so recently could theoretically happen again, I toggled between gratitude and fear.

I was grateful it happened so quickly, of course. I didn't have to experience that gut-wrenching disappointment—that moment of hoping to see a positive test and seeing a negative symbol instead—but getting pregnant on the first try, for me, came with its own set of complexities. It ultimately meant that I wasn't afforded much time or space to grieve, let alone cope with the realities of what it might feel like or mean to undertake another pregnancy. And even though this was a choice I'd consciously made for myself and our family, it didn't take away from the gravity of what I was undertaking. I had been pregnant for four months, then without warning, I'd spent the following four months not pregnant, then suddenly there I was, pregnant again.

This third pregnancy rendered me anxious to my core.

Being pregnant for a year and a half in total, with a break of four grief-stricken months, was an exercise in mind-numbing uncertainty—an ongoing oscillation between hope and anxiety. I was terrified for four of the nine months and on pins and needles the remaining five.

...

Considering how whiplash inducing this whole experience was for me, it wasn't hard to surmise just how overwhelming it was for my patients. The loss of my pregnancy brought with it a newfound set of professional quandaries, challenges, and most importantly, resonances. Now, to make matters more complex, I was a walking advertisement for pregnancy after loss. My ever-changing body evoked palpable feelings in those around me: envy and resentment, empathy and compassion, anxiety and wonderment, and unabashed hope. My body broadcasted where I was in my journey, and patients couldn't help but wonder if their experiences might mirror mine, and vice versa.

I disclosed to many of my patients fairly early on that I was pregnant again. Since I'd lost a pregnancy so recently, I wanted to be as forthcoming and transparent as I could with those who would take the news somewhat in stride. What's more, my petite frame revealed even the earliest signs of pregnancy, so I didn't want to leave them wondering on their own. Better for them to have the facts, I thought, than to be fixated on guessing about my pregnancy status.

Not everyone would take the news well, though, and I was well aware that my pregnancy might be burdensome for some and outright anxiety producing for others, so I held back from sharing with some patients until I couldn't any longer. The timeline was intense, after all, and bordered on triggering for some. I understood this, and knew I'd have to prepare myself for some difficult conversations. I didn't want my news to distract from theirs. I didn't want my belly to take up more room than it already was.

I vividly remember one particular session with Madison, whom I'd been seeing for several years. Madison had suffered two pregnancy losses—a miscarriage in the first trimester, another in the second—and had struggled to conceive in the first place. Upon walking into my office on that afternoon in early April, she noticed straightaway my larger-than-usual belly and confronted me—not aggressively, mind you, but forthrightly.

"Wait . . . you're pregnant *again*?" She looked at me with incredulity. "Sorry . . ." she attempted to backtrack slightly. "I just wasn't expecting that." She looked down at her feet while she unzipped her jacket and muttered, "It all just comes so easily for you."

Bump envy is something I hear about daily in my work. Looking in on other people's lives, it can be tempting to imagine that the path to pregnancy was "easy" for her, and her, and her. For everyone else. It can be tempting to assume that the beautiful, blooming baby bumps around you got there unscathed. But how can we know for sure? We can't, of course, but the appearance of pregnancy, coupled with the romanticized version of gestation often shown in media—be it television shows, movies, or social media—makes it far too easy for so many of us to deduce a person's reproductive journey by focusing solely on the end result. You are pregnant, therefore trying to conceive must have been easy for you. You have a baby, therefore pregnancy must have been easy for you.

From the outside, sure, it undoubtedly looked like I had everything back the way I wanted it; yet on the inside, I felt anything but steady. If we know the statistics, then it's actually safer to assume that the women walking by you whose bellies prompt an oozing of envy have stories of adversity all their own. Struggle is universal—manifesting in different arenas for all of us. We don't know what anyone else has been through, until we do. And even if my reproductive timeline looked enviable, pregnancy this time around felt like tightrope walking; there was nothing blissful or easy about it. It was rife with charged emotion that spanned both ends of the spectrum. I was grateful—elated, even—but no ounce of my joy was enough to counter the anxiety and fear I shouldered. It seemed as though my feelings would change by the hour; I felt petrified, hopeful, distant, excited, enigmatic . . . I don't know that there was a feeling I didn't have over the course of a single day.

My ob-gyn assured me that I'd likely find some respite after hitting the sixteen-week mark; but as that milestone came and went, it only offered a modicum of the equanimity I was so desperate for. I spent the first four months terrified that I'd lose the baby at any given moment; and even though an element of my fear eventually softened, I spent the remaining five months of my pregnancy walking on eggshells, expecting at each trip to the bathroom to see blood when I wiped. Even in spite of having received news that the fetal chromosomes were healthy, I couldn't shake the unmistakable fear that something could go wrong at any time.

With my patients' stories lodged in my psyche, I was all too cognizant of the fact that I was not immune to a repeat trauma. After joining that one-in-four pool, I somehow felt like any of the other horrendous reproductive statistical outcomes were somehow more likely to reach this pregnancy. It wasn't necessarily a helpful or productive way to think about conception after loss, I know, but a grieving mind has a way of meandering into dark corners—especially given the amount of anxiety that a postmiscarriage pregnancy can usher in. Beyond anything else, pregnancy after loss for me became a lesson—albeit one I wish I hadn't had to endure—in being present; to do nothing more than inhale, exhale, repeat. It was all I could do to keep from being swallowed whole by anxiety.

This practice of staying present was never more riddled than it was in the moments when I was home with my son. I was stuck in a perpetual state of worry, unable to untether myself from the overwhelming concern that my grief-shredded state of mind might color his childhood experiences. I'd find myself all too aware of my less-patient reactions to things that previously didn't push my buttons, things that all toddlers are wont to do. I felt like I could actually see myself in real time as I stretched to muster my previous ability to parent calmly. The trauma reared its ugly head in inopportune moments (not that there is ever an ideal time to be thrust back into this kind of havoc) and sometimes overtook my parenting strategies; I watched helplessly as that hallmark irritability rose in me. It felt, at least to me, like it was splintering some of our precious moments together, and I was so hard on myself about every time I thought I hadn't reacted the way I should have. The way my previous, pre-loss self most definitely would have.

This is the post-traumatic experience—our past remains ever present. Encumbered by the weight of our traumas, we feel the sting of every terrifying possibility. Worrying that my relationship with my son would be affected, worrying that something would go wrong with my pregnancy. Worrying. Constantly. *Anything could happen*, we think to ourselves. So why should we believe for a moment that the worst-case scenario won't? The naivete that perhaps existed for us in the past is long gone, replaced by an acute awareness of the risks and dangers that may or may not be dotting our paths, just out of our lines of sight.

Having experienced a miscarriage did not fortify me from having to face whatever horror the other shoe dropping could, or would, bring. I felt just as susceptible to any other type of loss, as though a new iteration of that familiar nightmare might be lurking around any corner. Day in and day out, I felt acutely aware of all the ways in which this pregnancy was so antithetical to the others: fraught with fear. So, seeing the effects of my two back-to-back pregnancies as they rippled through some of my sessions with patients was hard. I didn't want my personal life—my obvious and protruding maternal trajectory—to in any way affect my patients, of course, let alone hurt them outright. But in sessions like that of Madison's, perhaps I (or more specifically, my growing belly) inadvertently did. My conspicuous desire to try again—to attempt to grow my family once more—became a focal point for some, and stirred feelings deserving of my pointed attention.

· · ·

Even though I'm in support of women sharing their pregnancy news whenever they feel ready, there is a nuance to sharing about pregnancy early on—and particularly so for me, in my role as a psychologist specializing in reproductive and maternal mental health. I'm distinctly aware of how sensitive I must be in considering my patients' histories. No matter how delicately I shared my pregnancy experience—and share I must, at some point—it was bound to activate negative feelings in some.

But what better place—one might argue—to be triggered than in the safe and supportive context of your therapist's office? A space where feelings are addressed, talked through, and understood, together? Transference, a very basic and central concept of psychoanalytic theory, was bound to materialize during this period. And my work, now more than ever, was to take this in stride: to show up for my patients fully, to listen carefully, and to create a context in which all could be laid out and discussed. This was, of course, always the case in therapy, but given the fact that *I* was now part of *their* therapy process—my pregnancies, the lost one and the other that thrived, both activating feelings in them—my role had changed. Compassionate therapist though I still was, I now also carried the potential of being the problematizer too. We talked through all the feelings that arose.

But unfortunately, sometimes no amount of talking about feelings stimulated by this quick, next pregnancy of mine helped. To my dismay, one of my longtime patients, Paige, left therapy during this time. She'd been trying to get pregnant for years, to no avail. No pregnancies, no losses, and no children, Paige pivoted and decided to "give up" on family-building altogether. More than my bulging belly, it was the hope she saw in my eyes—later dashed and then returning once again—that pushed her to a place of intense discomfort in the context of my office, she told me. Hope that dissipated long ago in her eyes. Hope she held on to for years on end. Hope she loathed to see in others, especially now. So, sitting with me week after week became—understandably so—"more pain than it was worth."

I think of Paige, still. And I even hear from her on occasion. About thirteen months after Noa was born, I received a holiday card from Paige in the mail. The photo on the cover of the card was of her, her partner, and their newborn baby. In it, she shared their adoption story and her nascent impressions of motherhood, and reflected on our work together.

The bonds braided over years of weekly sessions can sometimes bring about a depth and emotional intimacy that—no matter the circumstances—prevail. I feel fortunate and honored that this was the case with Paige. Because, of course, it does not always work out this way. I am grateful when it does.

· · ·

Up until my loss, all I had known was my smooth pregnancy with Liev, and a steady clinical practice, with a specialization I knew only professionally, not intimately. Things changed. I became a person oscillating between hope and anxiety, trying desperately to foster the former while tamping down the latter as a grief-stricken wife, mother, daughter, therapist, and friend. In spite of knowing that my third baby was chromosomally healthy, the terror of loss continued still. Until she arrived safely, my daughter—and this thriving pregnancy of mine—felt more like a pipe dream than an eventual reality. And then, at long last, she came.

# 11

*"The discordant refrain of* what-if what-if what-if?*"*

My labor with Noa started gradually and progressed steadily. It rained that day, and I insisted on heading out on a hike in the hills in the early morning drizzle, with the hope of somehow getting things moving. By afternoon, contractions began, and as they quickened, my husband and I headed to the hospital.

Once we got settled in the hospital room, I recall hearing Jason talking with my doctor and the nurses, and moving about the room; I chimed in too. But the closer I got to the final stage of labor—transition—the more I required quiet and deep concentration. The intensity of the contractions demanded singular focus, most especially in those final hours.

I'd opted to forego pain relief. I had delivered Liev with the help of an epidural, but after experiencing the torment of delivering alone in my own home and the unmedicated D&C that followed, it became deeply important to me to bring this baby into the world while I was fully present, feeling it all. Soon after getting pregnant this time around,

I realized how poetic and powerful it would be if I had the chance to give birth without numbing, without taking the edge off. I hadn't really had an option as I labored through my miscarriage, but this time I'd have a choice, and I planned to embrace the pain willingly. There would be no fear of imminent loss this time. I wanted to feel my body go through this, and to bring about a new ending to the story I'd never intended to write at all. I wanted this birth— which I hoped would be a live one—to provide me with something reparative: the start of a lifelong relationship.

I spoke little, aware of the fact that if I left the steady confines of my mind, the physical pain might overwhelm me and propel me into another laboring direction altogether. The intensity of an unmedicated birth required stillness—I was in an internal, meditative state where I sat in silence on the birth ball. I stayed calm and quiet, inwardly facing the pain of childbirth with the knowledge that it was serving an important purpose—that each contraction was bringing me ever closer to meeting this baby of mine.

Pain is something we typically want no part of, be it physical or emotional, as it often signals that something is wrong, that something should be quelled. But not in this case. I went into labor with the mantra that in labor, pain is purposeful. Pain was a dance between my daughter's body and mine, a necessary conduit to her entry into the world. I stayed the course, and did what I could to shut out the uncertainty—the question of whether or not she'd make it, if she'd be okay. Loss, after all, has that way about it: colors are muted, sepia tones wash over what would otherwise be a bright(er) landscape. As the hours passed, I continued in my necessary retreat inward, focused on my breath. *This pain is purposeful*, on loop. Breathe. In and out. *This pain is purposeful. It is normal. Everything is okay*, I'd silently encourage. *I can do this*, I'd reassure myself. *We can do this.*

And finally, there she was. My daughter. Just after nine o'clock in the evening, midway through a strong push, sweet Noa Raye came into the world, curious and calm, and mere hours after a rainbow so fortuitously glowed outside the window of my hospital room. My rainbow baby. Here. Safely. The little being who'd spent the preceding nine months growing, thriving, and kicking about inside my body. I'd spent those months in varying degrees of unrelenting fear, but within moments of catching her and bringing her to my chest, the energy swirling inside me began to shift. I exhaled. Not all the way, of course. What I'd lived through to get here was as poignant and real as ever before.

Immediately following her arrival, Noa snuggled up on my chest and began suckling. I was in awe of her. I lay back on the hospital bed, my girl cozy in my arms, and drank in this surreal moment: her vernix-covered body, the sound of her breath as I fondled her little toes, and the fact that I'd actually made it to the other side of pregnancy.

About thirty minutes after Noa's arrival, the nurse brought her from my arms over to the counter to be weighed and measured. Suddenly, I was propelled back into a state of fear. I couldn't hear Noa. "Is everything okay?" I asked, panicked as the nurse weighed her. "I can't hear her. Why can't I hear her? Is she okay?"

Even though Noa had made it earthside, my angst pressed on. In fact, it instantaneously morphed into something else altogether.

"She's just taking it all in," the nurse said lovingly. "She's just looking around. Calm as can be."

Gobsmacked by these feelings, I was truly taken aback

that I was not in the all clear of these exhausting concerns, but I gently reminded myself to breathe. *She's here*, on loop, *she made it.* These compassionate thoughts rivaled the discordant refrain of *what-if what-if what-if* that I had expected would be quieted upon her arrival.

I was suddenly face-to-face with the realization that yes, she'd made it through pregnancy and into the world safely—*But how will I know if she'll last?!* It was unnerving to witness myself transferring the fear from pregnancy to newborn in real time: *Maybe she was safer on the inside*, I pondered. *Perhaps the pregnancy worry was a waste after all, and what I should have been even more concerned about was her staying alive upon delivery.*

I didn't see this coming: the next dimension of trauma. What I'd have to see through experience was the fact that what I'd thought was the finish line was actually the start of another marathon altogether.

I'd heard stories about sudden infant death syndrome and rare, fatal diseases of babies within the four walls that make up my office, but only now did those narratives make their way into my bloodstream via cortisol, into my now-deepening well of worry.

•••

As time went on and Noa grew little by little, the way I thought about my loss and the fragility of mortality morphed. With this darling daughter of mine earthside, I couldn't help but study her in deep awe, marveling about the fact that this beautiful person wouldn't have joined our family had my first daughter made it. Such a mind-bending, existential road I had found myself on.

Navigating motherhood in the wake of Noa's birth was, for a time, excruciatingly uncomfortable. It was as if a piercing alarm bell had gone off and was ringing at a pitch no one could ignore: the sound was a constant reminder about the vulnerability of life. No amount of thick skin could be located. It was all just too raw. *Anything can happen at any time*, I'd think. Where had my capacity for denial gone? It was one thing to parent Liev after my loss, but now with two little ones underfoot and a world of angst brewing inside, I struggled to maintain a sense of calm.

In those years when Liev was our only child, I was free of this great worry, but now, with two lives to raise and protect (and the loss under my belt), I found myself deluged by hypervigilance—deeply porous and more anxious than I'd ever been before. The cacophonous symphony of what-ifs was a constant, and fear-based thoughts popped in at inopportune times. Autopilot and denial eventually kicked in to help me master my days as a mother of two, but it took a while before I could quell the sound of those alarm bells that were ringing all too often, robbing me of the poise I'd had when I was a mother to one and no other. Post-loss motherhood: a whole different ball game.

• • •

As time moved forward and my feet steadied on the ground, I finally had the chance to fully relax—to unclench my teeth, release the morsels of antagonistic anxiety, and marvel at Noa's existence in a state of peace. I fell hard in love with her, and Liev was taking his newfound role as big brother in stride. I was feeling much more like myself and was well into the swing of my clinical practice again. I was back in the saddle. But on occasion, something seemingly mundane would flip a switch, and I'd find myself thrust right back into that post-trauma, distressed state of mind. Seeing this in my patients was one thing—I knew how to reassure them that what they were feeling was, in fact, normal—but when it was me, knee-deep in flashbacks or flooded by anxiety, I had a difficult time deciphering up from down, left from right, what was real and what my anxiety was manifesting.

Our grief doesn't dissipate overnight, nor are our feelings about what we've lost replaced by the overwhelming love of those resting safely in our arms. Life doesn't replace death. It doesn't need to, and it simply can't. And since the existence of one child does not negate the loss of another, why does culture—with its wonted way of focusing on happy endings—demand that we turn our backs on our grief to serve our well-being? We needn't succumb to this insidious unspoken pressure.

And so was the case with me. Noa's arrival was a monumental turning point, but the months that preceded her birth were sullied by an awareness that anything could go wrong at any time, and my resulting worry that surely something would, even after she entered the world. Noa's birth was pivotal and deeply healing in that sense, as was the subsequent opportunity to reflect on the fact that we'd made it through every single one of those harrowing weeks of her development, and that I'd done so without having to relive the horrors of what had happened to me such a short time ago. There'd been no blood, no early labor, no unassisted home birth, no traumatic loss. Instead, only the good, the predictable, and the expected transpired in that pregnancy and there in that hospital room. Noa's birth was physically intense, of course, but I had welcomed the opportunity to feel every twinge of pain. I'd gotten the reparative birth experience I'd yearned for and trusted my body through it. *This pain is purposeful.* I had the chance to be present in mind and body with a positive outcome, the way I was when the outcome was bleak, with no choice in the matter. An outcome so confounding it is still hard to find the perfect words to sum up. This time was different.

One of the most insufferable and surprising parts of grief is that one moment we can't stand to feel our sadness for another second, and the next we are scared of ever losing the intensity of that feeling. That somehow the passage of time, and the eventual lessening of the sting, is an affront to the memory of the one we lost. This thought pattern is common among the bereaved, but the dichotomy is even more intense after a pregnancy loss, because there are so few who *knew* the lost one—sometimes, of course, the pregnancy isn't even known until after the loss occurs. To let go of grief can feel like letting go of memory, and if we alone bear the burden of those memories, that can be a terrifying thought. So then why not allow grief to stay, even as time moves forward and joy returns? *The pain is purposeful.* I learned that I didn't have to choose.

In acknowledging that death is as big a part of life as birth, we recognize that sometimes intense gratitude and unconditional love commingle with fear, overwhelm, and angst. And in so doing, we let go of that strident, fantastical notion embedded in our culture that the birth of one baby somehow erases the complex feelings of having lost another. Replacement isn't a thing when it comes to pregnancy and human beings. We find, then, that it's imperative to extinguish the idea that the existence of good negates all that which has been painful in the past. Trauma is like tar, sticking to our innards, affecting so many things, from the way we physically move through our environment to the way we psychologically process the world. We must hold both. Even if we don't feel capable of managing both, we can and we will.

Moving into this headspace ever so subtly changed the way I practiced as a therapist. I relished the three-month maternity leave: to bond with Noa, to foster a connection between my children as siblings, and to familiarize myself with my reformed mind, now mothering two. In that still-inchoate time—milky and sleep deprived as I was—I knew that steadying my anxious tremor was paramount to a successful return to the workforce. Clearly visible in my rearview mirror was the hasty return I had made after my miscarriage, and I wasn't about to do that again. So I made sure not to rush. And I made sure to sink into this new life of mine—as a family of four—with the deep imprint of what had come before and the grief that was born of it.

• • •

When I made my way back to work, I felt well—a much-welcomed and marked distinction from the way I walked back in after my loss. Interactions with my patients felt measured, and I was back to being focused on their stories without a recent and similar narrative of my own hovering in the background.

Compared to the return following my miscarriage—that abbreviated moment where I hardly even took in what had happened—this time, in hearing their stories and sharing their grief, I felt sturdy. I felt encouraged and validated by the way my experience had changed me. My loss quite literally helped bolster my ability to understand and relate to my patients in ways previously relegated strictly to the theoretical. After Noa was born, sitting with my patients—no longer pregnant, with no plans to be again—I was able to sink into my work with aplomb. And, I noted, the fact that new patients meeting me for the first time would not have to encounter my burgeoning belly (or the chaos of my loss) no longer rendered me as a potential trigger for those walking through my door. This brought enormous relief. A new chapter was underway.

## 12

*"Sometimes rainbows follow storms.*
*Sometimes they don't."*

My mother-in-law's first pregnancy was smooth, much wanted, and a girl. Toward the end of her pregnancy, movement lightened. She told her doctor. He assured her that everything was okay. Upon giving birth, they learned that their darling daughter Chaya had spina bifida—a birth defect that occurs when the spine and spinal cord don't form properly. She died within ten days, never having made it to her crib at home. Bereft, my mother-in-law shuffled through the subsequent months in a fog.

A year to the day of the birth of her daughter, she gave birth to twin boys. My husband was one of them. My wonderful Jason. I am married to a rainbow baby.

•••

I wonder how many people are rainbow babies and don't know it. Pregnancy loss is a quiet epidemic—a circumstance that too many sequester. Since research has given birth order so much weight, I think it would be fascinating to widen the scope to include rainbow babies and the losses that came before. To investigate the impact previous losses have on the way we survive the subsequent pregnancy (if there is one) and make our way into parenthood. Are these children then treated differently than they might have been had their parents not undergone such a profound disappointment, resulting in pain and fear?

• • •

Claudia was thirty-eight weeks along, awaiting the arrival of her rainbow baby, when we began talking about the fact that she hadn't bonded with the baby in utero. Too scared to fall in love with the idea of actually raising this child, she held back. "What if she doesn't actually make it?" she said on countless occasions. "I've got to protect myself from the potential pain of losing this baby too. I just don't want to get too attached. Too close."

I hear about similar declarations daily in my work, as women make their way toward parenthood with understandable trepidation. There are times when the fear looms so large it gets in the way of the mothers connecting with their babies. Their hopes are shy—tentative even—but typically exist nonetheless. The fear of loving and losing once more feels untenable. Claudia is a single mother by choice and became pregnant through insemination. Her previous pregnancy abruptly ended at the tail end of the first trimester: a missed miscarriage. She'd fallen hard for being pregnant, having always wanted to be a mother. To make matters more complex, Claudia desperately wanted to raise a son. Her heart was set on it, as she imagined raising a feminist boy who'd be a kind and fierce leader in the world, helping to change concepts of stereotypical and toxic masculinity in subtle but important ways. This was her vision for a boy; a boy who didn't make it. Her loss was indeed a boy. Conflicted by feeling letdown upon learning her subsequent pregnancy was a girl, Claudia felt guilt burrow in, furthering the difficulty in bonding with her developing baby.

I've heard from many women about post-loss next-pregnancy "sex disappointment." This is yet another aspect of loss that seems to be shrouded in silence— shame, even— because the response women typically receive when they share their disappointment is something along the lines of "you should just be happy this pregnancy is healthy" and "at least you were able to get pregnant again quickly." We should be grateful. We should keep things into perspective. After all, things could be worse.

These dismissive statements often yield isolation and self-doubt, anger, guilt, or confusion. It's common to, when and if we find out the sex of a fetus, to imagine raising that boy or girl: fantasies that often rely on outdated gender stereotypes and the lingering gender binary, sure, but can serve as a bonding exercise nonetheless. We see what we hope to one day experience, and in doing so feel closer to the life growing inside of us.

If one has fantasized about raising a son, like Claudia had, for example, is one not allowed to experience sadness at no longer having the chance for that imagined future to come to fruition? Shouldn't parents be allowed to have and express their mixed emotions about this sensitive and deeply personal aspect of pregnancy and infant loss, and life after? Shouldn't anyone who has experienced a loss be given the space, and grace, to continue to mourn a future that was only given a chance to exist in their mind?

Claudia was met with bewildering responses when she dared to share her sadness and anxiety around having a daughter. What's worse is that some of these comments not only judged her disappointment in the baby's sex, but also skimmed the surface of her fear around being pregnant after her loss. She'd try to talk with loved ones about her reticence of bonding in case this pregnancy were to go away, and with no exception, she would be met with flowery, oversimplifying platitudes. Statements that completely missed the point and even served to minimize her fraught experience of pregnancy. "But it'll be different this time. Just be grateful." A statement that landed with a crass thump each and every time. And so, Claudia quieted her manifold, legitimate feelings, which quickly led her to feel ashamed of them. Anger scaffolded and led to an isolation previously unknown. "I feel like some of these people also judge the fact that I'm choosing to have a baby on my own. My family is very supportive, but it's been shocking that some of my friends think it's an out-there idea."

These same friends inadvertently misspoke after her loss as well—promising a concept that's actually faulty and unfounded: "You'll be okay, there's always a rainbow after a storm!" Is there, though? We all know this is not an unequivocal truism. Born of hope, this sentiment is simply not something one can ensure and therefore, we do better to shy away from blanket statements like these that don't always hold up. Perhaps people rely on these untruths in order to help themselves feel better amid the unknowns. In most instances, these declarations of certainty steeped in platitudes are well-meaning and the unavoidable outcome of people simply not knowing what to say in the lingering aftermath of loss. As a culture, we're woefully ill-equipped to handle even the concept of death, let alone discuss it outright or linger in the myriad ways in which it shapes us. So, in the absence of understanding, people say hollow things with the best of intentions.

But shouldn't they know better? Shouldn't we, as those who have been touched, changed, born anew by loss, demand better? Don't people know that rainbows don't *always* follow storms? That sometimes, all that follows is destruction, mortality, and destitution?

Blindly relying on the comforting notion that every traumatic storm is followed by beautiful, awe-inspiring happiness is common within the pregnancy- and infant-loss community. But we all know this isn't always the case. Some people don't go on to get pregnant again. Some get pregnant and have yet another loss. Some stop trying to conceive altogether. So while this hopeful message is encouraging for some, it might feel alienating to others, and in ways that are not always obvious. So many of us require more than the promise of a happy ending. Alternative outcomes—outcomes that do not consist of full-term pregnancies and babies wrapped in rainbow-colored blankets—deserve to be acknowledged too.

It's more inclusive and in fact more accurate to recognize that sometimes rainbows follow storms. Sometimes they don't. The same storm might produce a rainbow for one, while others are still searching among the clouds, hoping for a glimpse of a vibrant blue or orange, yellow or red hue. A rainbow for some does not ensure a rainbow for others. Sometimes, the clouds linger. This is a more reasoned way of thinking about the complexity of reproduction, and specifically about pregnancy after pregnancy loss. Because, as we know, there are no guarantees. And we can't presume to know what is in store for someone else's reproductive future. We can barely know what will happen in our own. So it is wise to abandon notions of fairy-tale endings, since we can't know what's to come, and because, when you really think about it, things don't usually work out perfectly in fairy tales either. Compassion and nonbinary language surrounding this topic should take precedent. The last thing we want to do is create a feeling of Otherness within our own community. Sometimes a rainbow follows, and sometimes it doesn't. Sometimes a rainbow is a child, and sometimes it's the renewal of vows, a career milestone, a new sense of self, the ability to self-love. And, sometimes, a rainbow baby is not one that is carried by the loss parent, but is brought into the fold via adoption, surrogacy, or foster care. And even if a rainbow does follow the storm, there is so much we might wrestle with throughout pregnancy and parenting after loss. So much more nuance tucked in.

The next time I saw Claudia, her daughter was three weeks old. She brought her to our session, and as her sweet baby calmly nursed, Claudia told me about the labor and delivery process and how things have been going ever since. Still hesitant to fully sink into motherhood, she spoke of her simultaneous enormous love of her daughter and her detachment. As we waded through these ubiquitous feelings, I found myself mentally revisiting the unimaginable loss sustained by my mother-in-law.

She had not gone to therapy after the birth and death of Chaya. She didn't have much support. So how did she fare? Was she afraid to get pregnant again? What was she thinking and feeling throughout her pregnancy with her twin sons and in those early days after giving birth to them? How, if at all, did those thoughts and feelings affect the initial period (or even the long haul) of parenting? Did she feel alone?

These were things I hadn't thought enough about until that moment in session with Claudia. Just as I started to feel guilty about never considering these questions before, my focus returned to Claudia and her little girl lying across her lap. We talked about her anxiety and how it swirled at particular times of day. We discussed how the vulnerability of being alive comes that much more into view after loss, and how this newfound look at mortality can hover during the transition to motherhood. It becomes difficult to whole-heartedly open yourself to this experience once you become conversant in holding back on hope. To believe it'll last. The perverse what-ifs might hauntingly make their way into the nursery. They might. Or they might not. For Claudia, they did.

· · ·

I fell in love with her at first sight. Noa Raye. I really did. But like Claudia and countless other parents who journey through pregnancy and parenting after pregnancy loss, I hesitated to open my heart fully, albeit unconsciously. Time, of course, has allowed for the softening of the past and the fear that came along as a consequence. But when I learned I was pregnant not long after my miscarriage at sixteen weeks, I was simultaneously ecstatic and terrified. I'm a lover of the state of pregnancy—through and through—but after my loss, I was awash with fear that translated into emotional distance—trauma's residue. *What-if what-if what-if. What if*-ing felt like a full-time job.

Parenting after loss can be copiously complex. It can range from the challenging—the piercing anxiety and the residual effects of PTSD—to the overwhelmingly positive, for what has allowed me to marvel at my children's existence at new heights I'm not entirely sure I would have reached without having experienced miscarriage. Before my loss, I think I'd really taken for granted the mere wonder of this fragile and unpredictable life. That blissful state of unknowing is long in my rearview mirror, and in its place now sits a magnified sense of wonderment over the lives of my two children and the loss that, to this day, lies in between. What was born from the mess of it all was the realization that immense gratitude and love can often and easily live alongside complicated feelings of grief and anxiety. Mothering can be complicated beyond our expectations, no matter how deeply we yearned for the role.

I was not the same kind of mother after my miscarriage. On one occasion, shortly after we'd introduced Noa to solid foods, she woke up from a nap spitting up in a way I'd never seen before. Instead of seeing this as a normal occurrence, cleaning her up, consoling her, and moving on, as I'd done so many times with Liev in his infancy, I panicked. This seemed different. I was alarmingly convinced that this could be Noa's end—that somehow she'd throw up again and again, that her body would purge its stockpile of resources, and then *poof*, she'd be gone. I called the pediatrician straightaway as I watched Noa go from her usual pinkish color to opaque to a camouflage green. I explained what had happened to the nurse on the other end of the line. She instructed me to hold Noa upright and monitor her as we remained on the phone together. The nurse compassionately listened to what felt like a big ordeal to me but was a small one (if an ordeal at all) to her. Noa was perfectly fine—thankfully, she resumed normalcy within a minute or two—but this was the turning point that alerted me to the fact that maybe I was not.

A few weeks later, as I drove along Mulholland Drive's winding curves on my way to work, I found myself keenly aware of the lack of guardrails along the road's steeper edges. I'd been driving this road without a second thought for as long as I could remember—music blasting, dancing in my seat, enjoying the glorious view—straddling the San Fernando valley and the hills of Hollywood. But on this particular morning, amid the clear, blue skies and the all-too-familiar surroundings, my mind veered from taking in the beauty to realizing it was possible I could actually slide off the edge. With these eerie and porous feelings encasing me, I had to coolly talk myself off the proverbial ledge as I continued along my drive to the office. But this disquieting experience drove home something unfortunate: the ubiquitous aftereffects of PTSD were still clawing on, showing themselves in ways that felt unbearable. Hard to swallow was the fact that this new stage—of mothering my little rainbow baby and her older brother—was accompanied by an intermittent, pervasive ticker tape of what-ifs.

...

Claudia wasn't aware of my loss history. Not to my knowledge, anyway. When she came to therapy, I was already out of the baby-making phase of my life. It's possible she was privy to my writing on the topic of pregnancy loss, but we hadn't discussed it face-to-face. I was struck by how different this felt, how interesting it was, to sit with Claudia (and other newer patients) as she (and they) often described feelings I knew too well in my own life, but which I had good reason to believe they had no clue I could precisely understand. I *got* them in a way they might not have known, or ever assumed. What a different phase of my career this turned out to be.

With my specialty area now bound to me corporeally as well as metaphorically, I was rendered uniquely able to identify with my patients in an entirely different way from before. For better and for worse. I'd pursued emotional work; I knew that from the get-go. I loved the idea of sitting with people as they bravely poured over the particulars of their lives—making meaning, solving relational riddles, exploring long-held beliefs. But what I didn't know was that a handful of years into private practice, my work would no longer be nebulous or simply the stories of others. It would now be my story too. If patients ask about this area of my life, I tell them. But if they don't inquire about my personal experience with loss in motherhood, I keep it to myself.

When Claudia's daughter was just shy of four months old, Claudia made an important decision. A well-thought-out one. One she had been hesitant about since her daughter's birth, when it weaved its way into the ruminating thoughts as yet another anxiety-producing thing to consider in this nascent transition. Her anxiety hadn't let up. In fact, it had only worsened. Sometimes, time alone does not make a dent. And sometimes, talk therapy isn't enough either. Sometimes, something more is necessary. In this case, it was. Claudia decided to pivot and try something new. She started medication, under the care of a perinatal psychiatrist I recommended after seeing how deeply she was struggling.

Within six weeks of taking the prescribed SSRI, Claudia described feeling like herself again. The medication sufficiently cut through the anxiety, and though the initial side effects were off-putting, the benefits were substantial. The constant loop of what-ifs faded into the background and eventually fled the scene completely, allowing her to relish more subtle and enjoyable feelings, like joy and contentment—giving her access to being more fully present. She was still human, of course, and experienced the expectable ups and downs, but since she was no longer lambasted by unruly thought patterns, things were looking up. She'd been tentative about going this route, but now that she was reaping the benefits, she was more resolute than ever that this was in fact a wise move.

The stigma associated with attending to mental health in our culture is chronic. Talk therapy is troubling to some, yes, but oftentimes, medication is even more taboo. Seen as a stealth thing, taking pills is often done in private and shared with no one, or if revealed at all, it's done so sparingly. I could relate with Claudia in more ways than one. I'd been there too.

After my Mulholland Drive incident, I knew it was time. It was time for me to address my anxiety in more ways than one. Talk therapy was grounding and illuminating, but it wasn't able to affect my biology the way my anxiety was unabashedly screaming to be addressed. Too many incongruous instances were now under my belt. I had mixed feelings about starting medication, though. I bargained. I kept hoping time would do the trick and I'd get to skip this step.

The biggest stumbling block—which I perennially used as an excuse—was breastfeeding. I half joked that Noa might've wanted to nurse until heading off to college—that's how much she enjoyed that bonding time. I didn't want to stop. I loved our time snuggled up together like that too. Noa had been eating solids for a long time—she was in no way reliant on my milk for sustenance—but I knew that if I were physically near, she'd inevitably yearn for the breast. For comfort and closeness. And I'm sure I would've wanted that, too. I thought that push/pull might rev up my anxiety all the more. Although SSRIs and breastfeeding can safely happen in tandem, considering this option became yet another source of anxiety for me. My chorus of *what-if what-if what-if* played on loop about this too. About traces of medication she'd possibly be exposed to, about what this could mean for her health, about my role in it all. It felt too delicate and too difficult to decide.

Finally, sick and tired of gritting my teeth to get through it, I asked friends how they'd gone about this transition (since Liev weaned on his own at sixteen months), and promptly took their suggestion to step out for a couple of days to change up the pattern. I booked a hotel room and, after twenty months on the breast, I weaned her over my birthday. It worked. Not without its associated feelings, of course, but it did work. And it was then—when my breast-feeding days were up—that I started an SSRI, with the hope of puncturing the what-if cycle once and for all. It took time, but it happened. The softening of my senses and my perceptions of them was palpable, and like Claudia, I felt much more like myself again.

Anxiety has the capacity to temporarily steal joy. It can wrangle the mind—baiting it to singularly focus on negative possibilities, whether true or false. In so doing, anxiety surreptitiously stomps out a spectrum of other feelings that actually exist simultaneously. A tough way to mother, it was quite a relief to have nuance back and to reconnect with ease and calm once more.

· · ·

Opal came to see me after learning she would not be able to carry a baby. She'd been diagnosed with a unicornuate uterus—a type of congenital uterine abnormality. She found this out the hard way. She was twenty-four weeks along in her first pregnancy when her baby's heart stopped beating. After several doctors' appointments and an eventual X-ray, it was clear she wouldn't be able to safely proceed in getting pregnant again. As if grieving the loss of her son wasn't difficult enough, now she was faced with a whole different kind of grief entirely: the loss of future pregnancies. "You'd think losing my son would make me exempt from additional heartache, but no, now I've been slapped with this other horrific piece of information about my body that means grieving pregnancy and the chance to give birth altogether. Loss piled on loss. It's all just too much. I can't win. It's so unfair."

I've heard similar thought processes numerous times over the years: the notion that a major hardship should somehow prevent future ones. I could relate, as I felt a variation of this way, too, after my loss and into the next pregnancy with Noa. *There's no way I can endure more. Lightning does not strike twice. It just can't.* But it can. And sometimes it actually does. And it's quite clear that no one is keeping score on the severity of trauma or the amount of it that each individual can endure.

"I used to think God had a plan, but how could all of

this be part of *my* plan? Or his plan for me? What could I have done to deserve this?" Opal wondered, simultaneously enraged and defeated. Sometimes religion and spirituality seem to anchor people as they attempt to make sense of their tragic losses—providing a belief system amid the chaos, a sense of connection and community, or a linear pathway for thinking about life and death. But what happens when the betrayal of one's body, as in the case with Opal, feels so incongruous with these long-held beliefs, or upends a lifetime of thinking that things were one way, then they turn out to be something else completely?

Opal has been dead set on being a mother ever since she was little. She talked about her childhood with fond memories, filled with daydreams about mothering in her eventual adulthood. As a kid, she practiced. When she played with dolls, she almost always appointed herself as the mother among them. And within her family of origin, Opal had taken to mothering her younger siblings ever since she was old enough to change diapers. When she grew older, Opal was a conscientious student and relished a fruitful career, but she shared with me that motherhood was the role she wanted more than any other. Several months after her stillbirth and the subsequent news about the shape of her uterus and its implications, she and her partner began researching surrogacy. An option previously not on her radar—not in her wheelhouse. She didn't come to this easily, as she sorted through conflicting feelings—based on her faith—about creating embryos she may have to destroy. "I feel like I'd be playing God and that just isn't right. It goes against my beliefs. What if we get loads of healthy embryos and we only use two? Then what?" she said as she reckoned with next steps.

She proceeded with the injections, supplements, acupuncture, and two rounds of IVF. From these, she got five healthy embryos. She'd envisioned having three children, and this remains a thorn in her side: having to—at some point—decide what to do with the extras. Opal's grief hovered over her through this period of her life, as she desperately missed the son she didn't get a chance to mother. But she tried to convert this energy into hope during the "two-week wait." They'd chosen a surrogate, done the procedure—transferring two embryos—and now Opal was on pins and needles awaiting the outcome. That two-week wait until pregnancy testing: a nerve-wracking, pregnant pause.

Opal reported that she stayed busy and tried to distract herself. She turned to prayer mostly, and met with her priest. She didn't want to stress over this, but it was inevitable. Those two weeks, she told me, felt more like two excruciatingly long years. Opal was scared that it wouldn't work and also scared that it would. She was scared to be faced with yet another pregnancy loss. She was scared, most of all, of allowing hope to spike   if the results were positive—with no guarantee pregnancy would last.

When she received the call from her doctor with news, she was trembling. "I literally couldn't speak. I was so overwhelmed by my emotions. I had so many. I just wanted to know: Was it a yes or a no?" She wanted more than loss motherhood so badly. She didn't want her maternal story to begin and end with stillbirth, but understandably feared it might. Opal constantly worried this would be the extent of her parenting experience: giving birth to a twenty-four-week-old baby who never took a breath in the world, never cried, never crawled. She recounted how she threw the phone to her husband, flustered, as the doctor began to speak. Too overwrought to listen in on the conversation, she intently scrutinized her husband's body language to see if she could surmise if the news was good or bad. It turns out it was both.

The surrogate did, in fact, get pregnant, but she was pregnant with a singleton, not twins. Awash with mixed feelings upon learning one embryo was thriving and the other was not, Opal took time to digest this information. But as the weeks ticked by, she eventually settled into picturing a healthy singleton and had her heart set on it.

Opal's son was healthily born without a hiccup. She'd struggled throughout the pregnancy process, but she got there. The birth was seamless and standard, and as soon as the surrogate pushed him into the world, Opal recalled how she burst into tears—tears that streamed down her face, landing gently on her son's as he cuddled into her chest. Utter relief filled the room and, at long last, Opal began a new type of motherhood odyssey. With a cooing baby in tow, tiny toes to tickle and marvel at, and diapers to change— as she'd practiced so many times with her siblings—she'd finally reached a destination she had imagined for decades.

Back in session some weeks after the birth, she reported that despite her dreams finally coming to fruition, she felt nothing. She loved her baby through and through, but couldn't locate herself. She was all smiles in front of friends and loved ones who came to visit, including her partner, but on the inside she felt empty. Vacant. Zombielike. Quick to anger, unable to sleep, and lacking in appetite, Opal felt inadequate and hopeless and wondered how it was possible she felt this removed from a life she'd wanted for as long as she could remember. She turned to exercise, meditation, church, and therapy. She turned to her midwife, a doula, and vitamins. We spoke about how common it is to experience postpartum baby blues, but we also talked about the fact that her symptoms were worsening with time, rather than clearing up.

Known as the most common complication of childbirth, postpartum mood and anxiety disorders affect approximately 20 percent of women in the United States.[22] Unlike the baby blues—seen in over 85 percent of new mothers, fading within two weeks' time—postpartum mood and anxiety disorders do not go away on their own. In fact, left untreated, postpartum struggles can turn into intractable longer-term issues. Given Opal's family history of depression, the twenty-four-week stillbirth, the grief surrounding not being able to safely get pregnant again, her conflicted feelings about IVF and embryos, and the fear that accompanied the surrogate's pregnancy, it made sense that she was struggling. We discussed her feelings at length and monitored their course. We talked about her expressed fear of not being a "good" mother, and the nagging, persistent feelings of guilt and worthlessness. We talked about her desire to withdraw and the eerie feeling of numbness encapsulating her morning, noon, and night. She'd been emphatically opposed to considering medication when we originally discussed it, but as her symptoms persevered and her concern proliferated, she opted to revisit her next steps.

· · ·

Sometimes, no matter how much we yearn for the role (or how ambivalent we are), the transition to motherhood is anything but linear. Particularly with a pregnancy loss (or several) under your belt, the imagined and hoped-for fluidity might not necessarily unfold in a straightforward way for loss moms. Be it anxiety or depression, or something more or less severe, mothering after loss can present unexpected twists and turns. And sometimes it doesn't. Sometimes it's smooth and ebullient. But either way, I think there is a need for pointed attention about maternal mental health when it comes to pregnancy after pregnancy loss and the potential emotional complexity that can arise in motherhood.

I think about the millions of people who have lost pregnancies and how they fare afterward. I think about the struggles that go unnoticed or unattended to. I think about how all-encompassing the role of motherhood can be. And I think about the vital importance of the mother's well-being inside (and outside) of the dynamic with her baby. A mother's emotional prosperity can help establish and ensure a fruitful attachment and a thriving relationship. Babies rely on parental attunement, mirroring, and consistency in care. This informs how they come to understand elemental things like love and trust. These building blocks pave the way for how they interact and interpret behavior in future relationships. And so, it is necessary to take your emotional temperature no matter how sure you are about motherhood. No matter how badly you wanted to become a parent. No matter how much you love your child. Because as humans, we are vulnerable. We are not impenetrable. We are affected by what came before. We are shaped by our experiences. And life has a way of throwing us off course sometimes—which can include pregnancy loss but also might show itself within the parenting landscape afterward. Whether you look in the mirror in those early days of motherhood and are all ear-to-ear grins or can barely even recognize yourself—barraged by disquieting, unexpected feelings—you are a mother. Don't discount your feelings. Don't minimize them. If you don't feel you can do it for yourself, do it for them. Do it because you now have their eyes looking to you, and because what we model in the way we take care of ourselves (or don't) matters.

...

Once my own anxiety softened—and then at long last, evaporated—I found myself back in a sturdy place from which to parent. Free from darting thoughts of worry, I embraced Noa's place in our family and was all the more present in my interactions with Liev too. This took time. It took effort. It still does.

Even something so pure and simple as my daughter's unconditional love was not immune to the far-reaching reins of my trauma. This is a situation many rainbow babies may not even know they've found themselves in—or that they've survived. But oh, how grateful I was to have transcended it. I often think about a phase she went through as a toddler—when she was firmly in a period of wanting to be glued to me, as if she wished we could literally merge. She wanted me by her side at all times. It was as if she remembered where she originated. This rainbow baby of mine truly makes me yearn for a pause button; a way to stop, or at the very least slow, the passage of time. Sometimes she stares at me with a knowing look, takes my face in her hands, and says, "Mommy, I grew in your body!" as if to express gratitude that everything went smoothly. As if she's proud to have formed inside me. We made it. This girl, this love, this peace. We made it. And although life brings countless opportunities for distractions from emotional intimacy, I still want nothing more than to cozy up with this sweet one—to giggle, explore, gnaw on her edible feet, and live off of her soul-healing cuddles. I want to have forever with her, endless opportunities for us to learn together. She, no doubt, is a teacher. My teacher.

In anticipation of Noa's first birthday, I wrote a mini ode to her. An illustration of what led to her and what has ensued since. I don't know when, or if, I'll ever show it to her. But I reread it often, reflecting on the rainbow that glowed over the hills of Hollywood as I labored, the one that held such significance, that yielded a sense of corporeal calm. I wrote of pushing her into the world, moaning with hope and fortitude. I transcribed the feeling of deep connection to her as I exhaled the fear that accompanied my pregnancy. I want her to know, in no uncertain terms, that I treasure the emotional roller coaster that led to her. I did not want it, but now that I have it I wouldn't trade it away if I could.

I believe that, on some level, my darling girl somehow just knows. One morning she pranced out of her room, excitedly snuggled into bed with the rest of my brood, and said with unwavering pride, "I'm grateful for my family!" My son promptly kissed her all over and exclaimed that her feet smelled like cupcakes; my husband giggled and took her into his arms; I simultaneously welled up and grew a huge smile on my face. This is the unique place that rainbow babies occupy in families: in a way, they carry the complexity of grief we felt as well as the relief we might now feel. That is the bittersweet beauty of rainbows.

## 13

*"Things. Things to have, and to hold,*
*and to see, and to treasure."*

After the dreaded unmedicated D&C procedure was finally over, anchored to a reality I could barely comprehend by unruly smelling salts and salted crackers, I watched as my body slowly but surely stopped shaking. I'd lost a lot that day: a baby, a great deal of blood, an imagined future, not to mention any remaining shred of innocence I was privileged enough to still have had at forty years of age. My body reeled. My psyche too. I was taken from my doctor's office and out of the building to our car in a wheelchair. Concerned about the possibility of me fainting from the significant blood loss, the doctors wanted to play it safe. And before I could fully embrace what had been taken from me, we were headed home—prescriptions in hand and a sip of juice to help stabilize me. Her remains stayed behind, to be sent off to the lab and analyzed. All we had were snapshots. Of her brief existence—of this liminal space we found ourselves in. Nothing more.

We took heart in knowing the fetal remains would be tested, to help determine why this unwonted experience happened at all. But that was all we thought to do. We didn't think to ask about cremation, a ceremony, a memory box. Miscarriage doesn't precipitate these conversations in the medical setting—about handprints, ashes, or funerals—whereas stillbirths often do. If I had experienced a stillbirth—the differentiation between these traumatic losses delineated by just four weeks, as the stillbirth term is applied to pregnancies at or past twenty weeks gestation—these options would have been presented to me. But due to what, at the time, felt like an arbitrary timeline, I was left without any tangible courses of action. No way to memorialize the life lost, save what occurred in my mind. My husband and I knew we'd be getting a call from my doctor in a couple of weeks, after she'd obtained the chromosomal testing results, but otherwise, I didn't even consider thinking about anything I might get to have or hold. Something tactile. Something sacred. Something that signified that this experience *really* happened. Honoring my loss or getting some semblance of closure around it was the furthest thing from my mind. I was still back in the bathroom, with the blood and the echoes of my primal scream and that godforsaken plastic bag. I was still just trying to survive.

Once my mind was able to focus on more than the sheer need to persevere, I contemplated things I'd heard and read about on the topic of honoring a loss. In my own Jewish culture, loss is seen as a normative, albeit challenging, outcome of pregnancy. For example, traditionally, many Jewish families don't give gifts meant for unborn children (including abstaining from having baby showers) because these items could be a painful reminder if the pregnancy is lost. Despite customs that acknowledge the very prominent *possibility* of loss, Judaism's position that life begins at birth leaves grieving families without standardized rites and rituals to honor a pregnancy loss. As I ruminated on my own culture's traditions, I thought back to patients like Opal, whose faith was a consistent, guiding presence in her life, even when her belief in God resulted in feelings of inadequacy and guilt. I felt, in a strange way, almost envious that the role faith played in Opal's life gave her, at the very least, a framework for processing her feelings; her questions about motherhood and fertility were, ultimately, a part of her relationship with God. It seemed that she, and others of similar convictions, believed that if they continued to focus on that relationship, healing through and from grief would come as a reward. While I'm not expressly adherent to the religious tenets of Judaism, I do find value in the customs. Knowing then that culturally, Judaism had little to offer in terms of schema and guidance, added to my already-frequent feelings of isolation in the wake of my loss. I yearned for comfort—and wondered if faith could provide some, like it did for Opal—but when it became clear it could not, I looked further afield.

And so, as I began to search for ritual, I let this be a moment to meditate on the nature of theological perspectives and reflect on how other spiritual codes choose to interpret and memorialize loss. For some, like Opal, there is an idea that loss, like everything, is part of "God's plan." This sentiment and its theological underpinnings didn't resonate with me—why make something so heartbreaking into an experience God would have a hand in? "Everything happens for a reason" is another phrase that gets repeated in some spiritual circles. To this statement, my retort is a diplomatic "does it?" It's a natural question, of course—one I had myself and that I parsed through after I read Rabbi

Harold Kushner's seminal book *When Bad Things Happen to Good People*. When Kushner's three-year-old was diagnosed with a degenerative disease, he was faced with one of life's most difficult questions: "Why, God?" As a result, Rabbi Kushner penned an elegant contemplation of the doubts and fears that arise when tragedy strikes. This text is a profound offering for those examining these philosophical dilemmas.

I've witnessed the many ways in which this question—"Why, God?"—can both aid and impede a person's healing process after a pregnancy loss. Opal, for example, felt like she was "playing God" by utilizing IVF, the underlying message being that this experience—pregnancy and whether it was successful, the number of children her family was destined to have, when she would become a mother—wasn't hers to determine. A higher power (the Christian God, in her case) was in charge of these reproductive outcomes, so seeking these medical options felt like an act of defiance, a deviation from God's plan.

In Judeo-Christian scripture, God rewards the unwavering faith of a follower by granting her the ability to have children despite her being barren. "And by faith even Sarah, who was past childbearing age, was enabled to bear children because she considered him faithful who had made the promise," reads Hebrews 11:11. Such messages can evoke feelings of inadequacy in people who are unable to get and/or remain pregnant. If God grants conception to those who are faithful, what does that say about religious women who are infertile? Who experience pregnancy loss? Who give birth to a stillborn? Religion and religious teachings can perpetuate the idea of "worthiness"—of who is, in the eyes of God, deserving of parenthood.

These edicts can also lead to a rift in one's relationship with religion. Instead of being a source of comfort, it becomes a source of uncertainty. If God "causes" miscarriages, or at the very least allows them to occur, is this otherwordly being worthy of devotion? If our chosen faith is unable to carry us through grief, should we continue to live a life in service of that religion?

Of course, religion can also be an important way to help make sense of things that don't make sense. The promise of an eternal afterlife in which parents are reunited with those they miscarried or delivered without breath can act as a beacon for those adrift in a sea of mourning. They are fueled by the knowledge that they will be able to love on the babies they lost once again. And in cultures steeped in specific religious teachings, the relationship with death and how the dead are honored can also provide comfort and hope. One can look at Mexican culture, for example, as a way in which death is not considered final, but an inevitable transformation of sorts. Practices such as Día de Los Muertos—the Day of the Dead—encourage and honor the constant contact between the living and the deceased. There's a palpable relationship with those that have passed, one that is cultivated with great intention and reverence. And within these practices exists a gratefulness to God for allowing those who have passed to continue existing in connectedness with those they have left behind.

Religion can also be an important source of guidance, since spiritual leaders may act as grief counselors, consoling loss parents via scripture and providing another layer of support, especially essential for those who may not be able to afford or have access to other mental health services. In a congregation, there often exists a deep sense of community, and in times of trauma that community can provide meals, perhaps even child care if necessary, or simply distraction and a chance at reprieve. Religion and spirituality can and do provide another avenue to assist us in becoming reunited with our former, pre-loss selves, and better acquainted with the people we've become in the wake of pregnancy and infant loss.

...

Outside religion, I continued my search for concrete ways to memorialize my loss, looking to individuals in my life, scouring social media, and listening intently to patients as they spoke of theirs. People seemed to honor their losses in such meaningful, sometimes elaborate ways. But I wondered, *Am I allowed to do the same?* I straddled the line between an early and late loss, so what should this mean about the way I ritualized this experience (or did not)? *Is this something that suits me? Honors her, me, us? Jewishly, does this feel resonant? If so, how? If not, why?* I was pummeled by the options and by my thoughts on the matter. I wasn't yet sure.

I gave myself time to marinate. There was no need to rush. And since I got pregnant again so quickly, there wasn't much space to dig into these ideas. My head was trying its best to wrap itself around this next pregnancy and the hope I could muster that it would, in fact, last.

I was inspired by things I'd read online—Instagram posts, essays—about practices like naming. I seemed to gravitate toward basic, gentle acknowledgments most of all. Giving a name to a lost baby as a way to legitimize the dream of them, the time spent with them in utero, and the burgeoning attachment to the idea of their very existence seemed compelling. This idea grew more and more appealing in time. It seemed like such a profound way to acknowledge in a small way something so major. Through this simple act, there is a powerful way in which we capture and concretize the fact that they were there, even if ever so briefly. This not only seemed beautiful; it felt necessary.

So, three and a half years after my loss, and another pregnancy later, I named my would-be daughter. Liev had voiced wanting a sister before I had even become pregnant at all, and proclaimed that her name should be Olive. As I turned this idea over in my mind, it eventually crystallized: his would-be sibling would, in fact, be named Olive. I loved that Liev came up with it. And it seemed a perfect name for her, in its symbolism and its meaning. The olive branch is a symbol of peace. Of reconciliation. Olive trees thrive under duress, bear fruit for thousands of years, and as a result, have come to represent resilience.

All of this felt fitting, like another important step in my grieving and healing process. Such reparation I found in this eventual naming—in being able to actually call her something. In my writing about loss, I could now not only talk about my loss, but also refer to the being who spurred this fierce, nascent passion in me: to change the cultural conversation surrounding pregnancy loss.

This emblematic gesture became a profound acknowledgment of the family member who never made it (in body) to our family tree, but whose brief existence deftly required the best parts of me. My fortitude. My vulnerability. My idealism. My hardiness was tough to locate at times, but my ability to adapt was with me through it all. It is with me, still. She is with me, still. My Olive.

This was a concrete step in memorializing my miscarriage, though technically not the first. Every year, on the anniversary of my loss, I light a candle. I light a candle in memory of her—a meditation on the recognition of that life-changing event, and the woman I became as a result. With pointed attention, I think about that day and reflect on all that's transpired since. I think about whether or not she felt anything when her heart stopped beating; when she fell from my body. Did she feel pain?

On October 15 of each year, in honor of Pregnancy and Infant Loss Awareness Day, I also light a candle. In communion with the countless women living in every corner of the world who have felt some variation of pregnancy and infant loss. I think of us all. It's astounding to consider the millions of candles lit on that particular day, and for the same particular reason. It's an opportunity to memorialize globally, in unity. We remember. A deep ache we all have in common.

...

Sage began to detail the ways in which she honored her daughter, who was stillborn. My body heated up with envy. As the rain pounded the pavement outside, we sat across from each other in my hazily lit office, talking about death.

Sage had ceramic footprint moldings, hair clippings, and a headstone. She had a place to visit her baby and a ceremony to honor her short existence. She'd gotten several photographs with her daughter. Her family had the chance to hold her. They got handprints too. She'd go to the cemetery almost weekly, bringing flowers and books to read aloud. One day she brought a chocolate cupcake with sprinkles and sparklers. These rituals felt like the most compelling ways she could think of to mother her daughter, she told me.

My body gave me all sorts of information—most notably in my chest, ever so slightly affecting the cadence of my breath—as I intently listened while she spoke about the version of motherhood she traverses. As I drove home in the rain that evening, I worked to understand what my body was attempting to communicate to me about the feelings that were elicited in that particular session. My mind fiddled as the windshield wipers sloshed to and fro. I was determined to figure this out, but ultimately couldn't. Stumped, I slept on it. I'd felt that pang of envy in session, but wanted to understand its meaning, its roots, the nuance. Why, of all feelings, was this the one that landed in my lap while face-to-face with Sage?

It wasn't until the following week, when Sage and I sat together once again, that it finally coalesced. She had access to so many rites and rituals—so many thoughtful, loving ways to honor her daughter's brief life and the impact she'd made during it. Sage had access to a framework that outwardly legitimized her experience with life and death. She had her faith, her religious community huddled in close, a plot of land that she'll visit until the end of time. She'd had friends and family surrounding her as her daughter was buried there. Flowers, and prayers, and tangible things. Things to have, and to hold, and to see, and to treasure, to prove that her daughter in fact made her way into this world, even if only without breath. It wasn't until now that it dawned on me: I needed something more of Olive. For myself, for our family, and for *her*. Something more to normalize loss and its riotous aftermath. Listening to Sage ignited an untapped desire in me to create, to instate, and to demonstrate out loud that which was brewing inside. To represent in a meaningful way—through rites or rituals—the profundity of these liminal spaces.

The following week, I shared these reflections with Sage and had the chance to express how moved I was by the ways she mothered her daughter, and in so doing, the ways she mothered herself. And how she, perhaps, was mothering other loss parents who have yet to share with her that her acknowledgment of her daughter's life was a silent acknowledgment of other babies lost to miscarriage or stillbirth too. We talked about the scarcity in our culture of rites of passage surrounding untimely death, and the isolation this begets. We spoke about motherhood in the absence of a baby and how invisible she feels in it, especially amid the countless women who have babbling babies in their arms; who have valid complaints about the utter exhaustion of parenthood—an experience those like Sage wish they could endure.

This version of motherhood goes widely recognized—a motherhood that is celebrated, adored, spoken about ad nauseam, rarely truly supported but nevertheless paid endless lip service—whereas the other version, the kind with no baby to show for it, is not so much. Sage spoke about wanting to feel legitimized in the mothering she does—recognized, acknowledged, appreciated, even. Her motherhood is work, too. Her motherhood is tiring in a whole different way than it is for those with littles running circles around them. And so, memorializing seems vital. Through it, we might not only buoy ourselves in the throes of grief, but these rituals might also invite others into the very essence of what it feels like to be a loss mom, empty arms and all.

Hearing Sage talk about her frequent trips to the

cemetery— the hours spent reading nursery rhymes under a tall eucalyptus tree there on the dirt—and witnessing the pride she took in this encouraged me to think harder about grief traditions available to women. Our conversations got me thinking about our current cultural limitations when it comes to memorializing miscarriage, how these acts of mourning and honor may make those untouched by pregnancy and infant loss uncomfortable.

...

A couple of weeks after officially naming Olive, my son and I went on an overnight getaway during his spring break, with sand toys and his scooter in tow. We spent hours on the beach talking about how the Earth spins, how the sun rises and sets, how the water moves—the ebb and flow of it all. The mood was playful as we danced in the moist sand and the sun eventually tucked behind the mountains lining the Pacific coast. Listening to Liev's lines of thinking as we skipped rocks felt like a meditation on the past, beckoning me to reflect on all that had happened since his birth. I knew this boy before my loss. He knew me before it too. And oh, how I'd changed.

Moments in which the previous me emerges leave me wishing I could somehow rewind—to go back to pre-grief laden times. To the mother I was before her demise. Unencumbered. As we readied to head back to our hotel room, he dug one last ditch in search of teeny sand crabs while I wrote Olive's name in the sand. Fingers enlivened by etching each letter, I realized it was my first time writing her name. Olive. Within a moment, the tide washed her name away and off it went into the sea.

Woven into the fabric of our newly shaped family, Olive came and went instantly. But the length of one's life does not dictate their impact. Brief stays can surely make themselves deeply felt, can't they? A profound and mighty impression they do make. Writing her name there, in the Santa Barbara sand, felt significant. It felt weighty. In a way, it felt like she was there with us on that beach, the letters of her name standing in for the footprints that should have been.

I wanted more. Setting her name in the light-brown granules on the Pacific Coast made an impact. It shored me up. But the tides would wash them away, and it was then that it became clear: I wanted to memorialize and signify our loss in more ways than this.

...

Soon, I turned my sights on Japan. I'd read about the unique ways Japanese culture acknowledges pregnancy loss and was eager to see for myself, in real time, on the ground, what it looked like. Zojoji Temple, located next to the Unborn Children Garden, is the resting place of six shoguns from the centuries-long rule of the Tokugawa shogunate. It is known for being one of the largest and most important Buddhist temples in Japan. Originally founded in 1393, the temple relocated to its current site in the 1590s. Surrounded by Tokyo's Shiba Park, the temple grounds are said to be airy and spacious. This garden is specifically dedicated to those lost to miscarriage, stillbirth, and infants who didn't survive. People decorate statues in bright colors. It is a place people can visit even en route to work, as it's smack-dab in the middle of the city—integrating death into everyday life. I was yearning to experience a culture that had a healing ritual for this kind of grief, and this seemed like as good a time as any to go. So in the spring of 2017, I enlisted my dear Aliza, a friend I've known since my days in Boston—the same friend who recommended my therapist, Valerie—to travel with me to experience it firsthand. The week before departing Los Angeles for Tokyo, while sitting with patient after patient, it dawned on me that even though our culture doesn't have standardized ways of memorializing loss, my office (and countless offices around the world) has become a sanctuary of sorts. The amount of love expressed within those four walls could deem the space holy, almost. Although we exchange words during therapy sessions, there is an abounding sense of grounding meditation. Ritual in the making. Simultaneous to words, gentle breath. Lost babies spoken about and felt deep within our bones. This realization was a potent way to begin my trip.

Adventurous to the core, I long for cultural immersion, the tastes and smells of elsewhere, stories written on unfamiliar faces. But I hadn't boarded such a long flight since I was blissfully (and naively) pregnant with my son. Jason and I ventured to Australia and New Zealand with Liev in utero. How was it possible so much time had elapsed? And how had I stayed put for so long? Motherhood, miscarriage, grief, anxiety, pregnancy after loss—all of this grounded me. And by "grounded," I mean cemented me locally and filled me with dread when I dared to even contemplate leaving my babies. My wanderlust was negated by my need to stay close to them.

Sitting alongside Aliza, I felt a shift. I was ready to be doing this again, often. Aliza too. She is all too familiar with pregnancy loss herself. After four miscarriages, she brimmed with joy as she FaceTimed her son, adopted at birth over seven years ago. We are both loss moms. We are both working mothers. We were both in need of this break more than words can explain. It says a lot that we both blurted out in the airport lounge that this act—sitting uninterrupted for more than a few minutes—felt like a needed treat, a vacation in itself. This woman is a light, a revolutionary, a warrior. I couldn't have chosen a better companion to dive into what was sure to be a pool of complex and conflicting emotions as we set out to explore the Jizo-filled garden in Tokyo and the countless bunches of statues strewn throughout Kyoto. We are familiar with the loss of pregnancies—the extinguishing of dreams. We also have in common fierce hope and an intention to transform culture (even if only a little bit), born out of personal experience.

The morning after we arrived, my mind was abuzz, eager to head straight to the Zojoji Temple just below the Tokyo Tower, adorned with Jizo statues. Said to represent both human and deity, child and monk, with eyes closed, hands clasped in prayer, and serene facial expressions, these statues adorned in red crocheted caps stand in memorial of miscarriage, stillbirth, and infants lost. A public place—a place where people gather to honor and connect with what they've lost. I'd seen pictures of this garden online—the Sentai Kosodate Jizo, translated as the Unborn Children Garden—but now I would have the chance to actually visit and drink in its profundity.

After enjoying a traditional Japanese breakfast, complete with miso, grilled fish, rice, and pickled vegetables, we were on our way. It was categorically awe-inspiring. I couldn't believe I was actually there, a witness to the rows and rows of decorated statues representing the souls of unborn babies, those who died too soon as well as those yet to be born. For late morning on a weekday, it seemed to me there were quite a lot of people—women and men alike—paying their respects. Several generations ambling through this meaningful space. Just because. Because they could. Because this space exists precisely for this very reason. To visit with those who are no longer.

The pinwheels stuck among them spun, the birds chirped, and the calming smell of incense floated through the air. I choked up with emotion as I stood amid this powerful scene. Japan has a culture known for its humility; here, they grieve through action—grieve out loud, in the open—rather than hiding it, the way our culture is prone to do. The statues reveal ritual, protection, love, remembrance, beckoning pilgrimage. In our culture, research has found that a majority of women ask, "Why me?" My hunch is that in Japan, they don't. When loss is normalized and ritualized in tender ways, we are less apt to blame ourselves or wonder, "Why me?" There is an art to grieving there. It is honored.

I thirst for this at home. Women I spoke with in the garden said they visit often, some monthly. One elderly woman shared that she comes to pay homage to her sister that could have been—her mother's stillborn baby. She laid flowers and quietly prayed, gently touching the statue's face.

That night, as we lay around in our hotel room relaxing and getting ready to go out for a night of sushi and sake, I posted to the @IHadaMiscarriage account with a recap of my day. In lieu of one of the many photographs I took, I posted a piece of art of the Jizo statues, which I commissioned before my departure, and another with an illustration and the phrase "Empty arms, full heart" written in both English and Japanese. I wrote about the enormity of my experience and how much I wished we all had access to a culture where grief exists out in the open—amid the fresh air, accessible to all—not just gnawing and eagerly scratching within the confines of our bodies. And although I don't know this online community in real life, I know their pain intimately, and I brought it there with me and wished they could all gather there too. Despite the sixteen-hour time difference, I saw comments populate immediately and found so much connection in the reactions as I read through them. I was moved all over again. The people of Japan may have this spectacular garden to connect and recharge themselves, but those responses were a beautiful reminder that I have a place I can always go, too: my Instagram community.

Next was Kyoto, otherwise known as the city of ten thousand shrines. In Kyoto, at every turn, you're met with calm-faced Jizo statues—some cuddling up together, others surrounded by handwritten messages, most accompanied by mini flower bouquets. Death is honored, almost celebrated there, by incorporating it into daily life. *Can we aim to achieve this at home?* I wondered as I zigzagged through throngs of Jizos meant to maintain remembrance. I carried Olive's spirit through the meandering, historic roads chock-full of temples and shrines, honoring heritage and tradition. I felt her.

•••

Upon my return from East Asia, it became abundantly clear that my trip had marked a turning point in my post-loss life; namely, in the post-traumatic stress I experienced after my miscarriage. Those symptoms were alive and well during my subsequent pregnancy and flowed disruptively into the initial months of mothering 2.0. Though I had every reason to experience these feelings as I barreled through the next pregnancy, I just didn't understand how much I was struggling . . . until I wasn't.

The fact that I boarded a flight to Tokyo, left my children safely at home with Jason, explored for just over a week, and enjoyed every second of it felt like a *profound* victory over PTSD and the trauma that birthed it. It was an emblematic turning point. As I sat among the embellished Jizo statues in a culture comfortable with acknowledging loss, I had the chance to bid farewell to any remaining bits of hypervigilance, releasing the proverbial monkey on my back. I found unparalleled comfort in being surrounded by symbols of loss out in an open space, watching as people came and went, lighting incense sticks and closing their eyes in reverence. Outside in nature, surrounded by others who presumably knew a similar ache. The ultimate embodiment of serenity. This was rites, rituals, and representation of pregnancy loss in action—it all seemed so natural and revitalizing. To actually witness people honoring their losses in real life—not online or in print, but in real time— made a lasting impression.

· · ·

Back in America, I opened up a dialogue with the community about their loss rituals. Through these conversations, I met Zoe, whose son was stillborn at thirty-two weeks. After naming him, she began getting tattoos in his honor, to concretize this loss—to make real someone who had only been ephemeral, a life that wasn't lived, but which nonetheless existed acutely for her.

"The process of getting the tattoos was healing for me. The adrenaline felt during the process of getting them numbed the pain," she told me. She now has seven of them. "They became an invitation for people to ask about me and about my son. It meant that I could share my story. I have a strong desire to keep him alive, though he was born dead—for people to recognize his existence," she explained.

Another follower, Sivon, did not know she was pregnant until she miscarried. "A big chunk came out of my vagina while I was at home alone. I had to scoop it out and questioned, 'Do I flush it? Do I bury it?' We have no blueprint. How can we know?" And so Sivon flushed, feeling a wash of guilt sweep over her, one that periodically still does. "Months later, I realized that my baby's womb life needed to be honored. My body was feeling those emotions too. It was a journey that needed to be had. I got a mini statue of a woman holding a baby with a rose quartz where the heart is. I keep it by my bed. Since I was so newly pregnant, I didn't get to experience the joys of pregnancy before losing it. But I memorialize my pregnancy by acknowledging I *was* pregnant." Sivon told me she now has a five-week-old daughter. "I never want to pretend this pregnancy was my first."

Inspired by my trip to Japan and conversations like the ones I had with Zoe and Sivon, I decided to focus my efforts on memorialization for Pregnancy and Infant Loss Awareness month in 2018. I wanted to dedicate my efforts to loss-related rites and rituals and invite others to consider ritualizing, no matter how long ago their loss may have been. We deserve ways to honor who we were previous to the loss, who we are after, and the babies we have lost.

And as my own journey proved, it is never too late to

consecrate these feelings. I used the campaign to encourage women and families to find their own way of memorializing their losses, one that feels meaningful and personal to them. While there may not be a cultural standard or template for a ritual, there are touchstones that we can find familiarity and comfort in: Take photos. Make something concrete. Have a ceremony. Plant a tree. Honor the anniversary. When I spoke to women in the community, it was clear: we really do want to acknowledge our losses. The way we do it—the way we parent these beings who are no longer—is different, but we all do want it. Not just for ourselves, but for *them*.

. . .

Last year, a moment I had long anticipated arrived. Liev, aged ten, began talking about my work one evening as I was putting him to bed. I'd imagined the moment was imminent, as his inquisitive nature had blossomed all the more recently. A natural-born thinker, Liev is perceptive and thoughtful through and through. And as we parents craft the right way to teach our children about the topic of sex and conception, I was aware that I wanted to consciously invest some time in educating him about the possibility of loss, too. Sex-related conversations between parents and their children typically focus, firstly, on how *not* to get pregnant, and secondly, on the ease of reproduction—namely, on the live births that follow pregnancy. But if our children are being taught that sex (and other reproductive technologies) lead to babies, should they not also learn that some fetuses never make it that far?

Liev knew some of this already; because of my work, we'd

discussed it. But the specific situation of my loss was one I'd been waiting to share. Partially, I didn't want to burden him, and wanted to be sure that he was mature enough to handle something this complex. Also, a part of me worried he might inadvertently blurt the facts of my loss in his sister's face, telling her before I had the chance to do it myself. I didn't know the best way, how to broach it or how far to take it. Sharing any of these details and the resulting grief with my son felt deeply disconcerting and somehow also intrinsically sacred at the same time. *In time, I will share—when the time is right*, I thought to myself, trusting that I'd rise to the occasion if it came up. I would pick and choose carefully what to share and what to leave out, of course.

Ultimately, there's really only so much planning one can do for conversations like these. And then it happened. We'd been talking about our respective days, and he'd been curious to hear more about my work and the stories I hear there. He proudly tells people that his mommy is a "doctor of the heart" (so some actually think I'm a cardiologist, amusingly), and expresses intrigue in psychological development—the way our histories shape who we become. One question led to the next, and there in his bedroom, I shared with him how my work intersects with my life.

"Well, Mommy, at least you never went through what those women went through. Actually, though . . . I guess if you had, you'd be able to understand them even better."

Here we were, I realized. It was time. I seized the opportunity and let him guide our way through it.

"Well, sweetie, I did, actually," I said.

"Wait, what?!" he replied. "You did? When?"

I brought him back to the day it happened, and piqued his memory by reminding him about how he'd had his first-ever semi-sleepover that evening, and that this was what led to it.

He pressed further.

"She was a girl," I told him, "and I named her Olive." I explained that, at just three years old, he'd told me he'd wanted a sister named Olive. So I told him that since his daddy and I had loved the name as much as he did, we had decided to give her this name.

"That's the name I loved. I really love that name, Mommy." There was a pause. "Wait, so you wanted three kids?" he asked.

"No, my love," I explained. "Noa wouldn't be here if Olive had made it."

He understood and opined about how much he loves his sister before telling me how sad he was for me that I'd had to go through that.

"I'm sorry, Mommy," he offered. His questions continued: "Why do babies die too soon?"

"Sometimes it happens because the baby isn't healthy, like Olive," I explained, "and sometimes it's because of other complications."

"So the baby's heart is beating one minute, and then not the next? Does it hurt the mommy's heart when that happens?" he asked, curious and concerned.

"They hurt indescribably so," I told him.

"But what do the mommies do the next day? Without the baby?"

"They rest. They cry. They remember. They receive support," I replied.

And at that, he asked to feel my heartbeat, and offered to let me feel his.

What a milestone moment this was, sharing about my

loss with my older child. My tender-hearted son. Such connectedness was ushered in during this deeply important conversation between us. I can only imagine what it felt like for him to hear this, and the way his mind will tinker with this emboldened information over time.

This exchange precipitated several other conversations, piquing his interest in pregnancy, loss, and the ways families piece their lives back together afterward. It's thrilling to watch his mind work as he darts questions at me that even some adults have never asked. There's abounding empathy revealed in his every perceptive query; it just about bowls me over with pride and gargantuan love. It makes me want to eat him up. Talk for hours. The subsequent conversations frequently took place during car rides—en route to piano practice, baseball games, play dates, they just pop out. He'll spring a question on me seemingly out of nowhere, which reveals and reiterates to me how thoughtful his mind is and what a huge heart he has. Liev asks, unprompted, from the back seat: "Mommy, how old would that girl be now?"

Unsure what he's referring to, as just a moment ago we were talking about Fortnite, I reply, "Which girl, sweetie?"

"The pregnancy you lost. It's so sad. How old would she be? Because if Noa is five and a half, would she be like seven or something? How old was I when that happened?"

His love. His memory. It stays strong.

I hope conversations like these continue until the end of time. I hope that lines of communication remain open between us—about life, death, and these liminal spaces—always.

## 14

*"Sometimes, a witness is precisely what we need."*

A friend recently asked me how to get "past" grief. Her miscarriage had occurred less than a week before and she was desperate to know how to navigate the emotional muck. She wanted a compass. Decisive directions. A roadmap that would adequately pinpoint any potential roadblocks, cliffs, detours, or "works in progress." *Go due north for about a mile, then when you get to the bend, head west: you will have arrived.* If only.

I understood this desire too well: To obtain information or a time frame of future grieflessness. To have some concrete knowledge, at least, of what lay ahead. "Swim in it," I said with a tinge of trepidation, wishing there was a better answer. "We fear we might drown if we lean into grief. But you won't. You might feel like you are, but we won't let you." There was a significant silence—an empty thought bubble hovered between us as she digested my words. And then, almost immediately, tears of acknowledgment dripped from her eyes in reverie. Sometimes, a witness is precisely what we need.

As humans, we are prone to trying to rush through the tough stuff—be it mild psychological discomfort or a more extreme situation, like trauma or tragedy. And this makes complete sense, of course. Why would we want to be psychologically uncomfortable, for any amount of time? It simply doesn't feel good. As a result, we sometimes attempt to skirt the issue at hand and skim the surface of pain because we want to get *back* to feeling good. As much as we'd prefer to skip difficulties entirely though, we all know that life doesn't really afford us this opportunity. This evanescent luxury. It can't and it won't. And beyond this impossibility lies what we would lose if we were capable of sidestepping trauma, hardship, death, loss, pain, grief. Because when we attempt to stave off our personal truths, including the ones that hurt, we often inadvertently stymie our capacity for growth and resilience. We might, by the very nature of trying to fend off some of our feelings (i.e., the unpleasant ones), unwittingly clamp down on the juicy ones as well, feelings like joy and love and peace. And as a result, we are likely to find ourselves living a little smaller, loving a little less freely—out of fear born of self-preservation—with the sincere hope of staying safe.

It's intuitive and distinctly mammalian—this survival instinct. This is not necessarily a conscious decision, of course, or by design. Sometimes surviving is the best we can do. But sometimes, we can do more. In time. I've had the distinct privilege of witnessing basic survival evolve into a state of full-fledged thriving, time and time again, in a micro sense in the context of my practice and on a macro level online. It's why I do what I do—in my practice and in digital communities. It is an honor. A privilege. To be present in this revelatory season with women. By digging into challenging feelings, facing pain head-on—stumbling across enlightening epiphanies along the way and quite possibly some pitfalls too—we can be carried from elemental survival to a sturdier state of mind.

This brings me to the concept of healing—a word I hesitate to use too often when it comes to pregnancy and infant loss, as it by definition might hem us in or accidently diagnose a problem where there isn't one (or, at least needn't have a solution). It might imply that there is something unhealthy or damaged (or that we are damaged), and that something (or someone) requires fixing. Must we be "fixed"? Should grief have a time frame we must adhere to? And if we don't adhere to it, then we are somehow seen as an outlier, a renegade who is not healing? I don't think so.

Healing is defined as "the process of making or becoming sound or healthy again."[23] The concept has also been described as "the process of the restoration of health from an unbalanced, diseased, damaged or unvitalized organism."[24] Grief surely doesn't fit neatly into any of these descriptions, nor should it. It's one thing to talk about healing in the context of physical ailments. We can, for example, literally watch a scrape or a bruise heal in real time in a matter of days. Emotional healing, however, is anything but linear, and isn't best described as "diseased." Far from it.

Grief is natural. It is normal. A birthright. It's subjective and relative. And as any element of healing comes about, it does so slowly, and not steadily in the slightest—particularly when it comes to miscarriage, stillbirth, infant loss, or any other form of reproductive trauma. In fact, there may never be a getting-over of what happened to us, either by chance or out of necessity. We move forward, rather, with the pain inscribed in our psyches. Must we work to get rid of memory altogether to become "healthy" again? I think not. The weight of our losses might feel heavy one day and markedly lighter the next, but the memory remains. If it does, it does. If it doesn't, it doesn't. Neither is indicative of being more or less "healed" or "healthy." Neither is right or wrong. There's not necessarily a linear path that leads us out of our discomfort and into an unaffected state.

We might also compassionately absolve ourselves of the inclination to search for a silver lining. There might not actually be one, and that's okay. We need not feel pressured into finding bright spots when we just landed in the dark ones, and we mustn't succumb to this binary vision of adversity. Sometimes things don't "happen for a reason" and sometimes there isn't a cheerful way to look at a horrific or heartbreaking situation. Sometimes when we try to make sense of why *bad* things happen to *good* people, we find ourselves searching for meaning where there is none, getting caught in a manufactured duality. We can hold both. There is room and necessity for nuance, complexity, and gradation. We can be hurt and healing simultaneously. We can be grateful for what we have and angry about what we don't at the exact same time. We can dive deep into the pit of our pain and not forget the beauty our life maintains. We can hold both. We can grieve and laugh at precisely the same moment. We can make love and mourn in the same week. Be crestfallen and hopeful. We can hold both. And so it goes. We grievers might stumble upon these notions the hard way (I'm not so sure there's any other way to come face-to-face with them), but nevertheless, we work to integrate them and, in time, deftly tuck them in to our pockets as hard-won wisdom we might just get the chance to impart someday.

This is what I've learned—as a woman, as a therapist, as a griever, as a mother. Though "healing" might not be the most apt word to describe what happens to us after we survive pregnancy or infant loss, we aim to become familiar with our newly shaped lives. We rest in this strange and unfamiliar place. We do our best. We arduously wrestle with and try to predict what might come next. We wonder if we will ever be our (previous) selves again. We ruminate on the what-ifs. We might even become impatient with grief. We make plans, knowing they, too, might take a left turn, even though before we were most always certain they'd go right.

Maybe for some, the concept of healing resonates. Either way, what matters most is that we take a stance of unequivocal compassion for what follows pregnancy and infant loss. Lacking in self-judgment, we do our best to play it by ear and show up for ourselves in whatever it is we are feeling. We can't always plan it. Control is out of reach, ephemeral. We can't get "out" of grief or "past" it or even "through" it, necessarily. And crucially, we should not try to circumnavigate or dodge it altogether. We can exist in it, together. We already do, actually, by the mere fact that we are one in four (miscarriage), one in one hundred (stillbirth), one in eight (fertility struggles)—the list goes on. Statistics adding up to the millions means we are plentiful and robust. But until women no longer silently muse, *I am in this alone, I feel isolated*, and *Why am I the only one this is happening to?* our work is not done. My work is never finished.

We must challenge ourselves communally and individually to do our part to shift the narrative: be it by sharing your own story, checking in on a friend, or claiming your truth aloud despite the fear. Big or small, your effort and place in all of this matters. Whatever version feels right for you, do that. And then maybe stretch a little further the next time. Stretching the empathy might yield transformative change: empathy for yourself and maybe even toward a reproductive outcome unfamiliar to you.

Together, we have the chance to rewrite the reproductive-loss script—we already are, in fact—for grievers and loved ones alike. It's underway, this much-needed zeitgeist shift. Imagine if the reproductive-loss landscape looked and felt fully inclusive of the spectrum of reproductive outcomes; if grief were no longer conceptualized as something to do away with, but rather were respected as the wise teacher it is; if silence, stigma, and shame dissipated altogether, and we actively moved closer to uncomfortable conversations, rather than further away. Then, and only then, will society change form. Permeating culture, storytelling would— once and for all—replace silence, making as much room for heartache as it needs, in perpetuity. With no rush, no expiration dates, no comparing or contrasting, no turning in on the self. None of that. Instead, this newfound spaciousness would normalize the circuitousness of bereavement and reframe discussions around pregnancy and infant loss.

Make no mistake: this is radical. Our mothers and grandmothers, aunts and sisters do not necessarily know what this world looks like, and it may be a difficult mindset to adjust to. What we are creating, through our vulnerability, our stories, our deeply personal and yet magically universal histories, may stir mixed feelings: everything from resentment that they did not receive the same support we are offering to those who come after us, to old and unprocessed grief—grief they were not allowed the time nor the space nor the language to process. Through truth-telling and expanding the reproductive dialogue to include grief as a mainstay—as well as apathy and relief—a much-needed metamorphosis might just be in order.

*Your* story might be the very genesis of this. I dare you to find out. I am here, rooting you on and supporting your every step. Sometimes a witness is precisely what we need to be seen, to be heard, to be honored for who we are, exactly where we are. To be seen amid transformation. A transformation that is so deeply personal, so profound. What's more is if enough of us dare ourselves to speak up, then maybe, just maybe, we can collectively incite a cultural transformation. A revolution of reproduction.

I have learned an immeasurable amount from the women who have sat with me in these moments. Through these potent exchanges of emotional intimacy, I have been bowled over by both the beauty and the catharsis that comes about from sheer vulnerability, benevolence, and tenderness. These connections have been legitimately life-changing, and they so deeply reflect what happens when we allow ourselves to share with one another—candidly—about these harrowing experiences. I've learned that getting comfortable with being uncomfortable is part and parcel of the grieving process. I've learned that silence is suffocating and that shame strangulates. I've learned that community might be the very antidote to these insidious vestiges. I've also learned that magic lies in allowing ourselves to lean in to our pain. We don't drown. We have one another to buoy us. Several years ago, for one of the installments of the #IHadaMiscarriage campaign, I gathered a diverse group of women, and one of the things I asked them to reflect on during our time together was what they pictured when they envisioned a world where we have achieved the mission, where we have finally replaced silence with storytelling.

The responses should come as no surprise to anyone who has read this far: "I'd feel safe." "I'd feel at peace." "I'd feel inspired." "I'd feel empowered." "I'd feel liberated for the women ahead of us." "It would be so freeing." I've heard every iteration—the ongoingness of hope for a shifted loss landscape. It's unequivocal. We want the reproductive-loss conversation (and lack of it) to palpably change. It's indisputable. We want it. Millions of us. Whether it's one story at a time, or a slew of them shared all at once—we want to see cultural change.

Through normalizing the conversation around what is in fact a frequent outcome of pregnancy, we work toward never again hearing a woman in the aftermath of miscarriage say, "I feel alone." We know there is a way to meet heartbreak with abundant support and free-flowing dialogue, eschewing antiquated things like self-blame, guilt, and notions of body failure. If the pregnancy-loss conversation was all-encompassing and capable of holding space or nuance, and if the various expressions of grief were embraced as acceptable reactions to miscarriage and infant loss—if we, as a culture, would simply trust those who experience pregnancy to name, express, and own the many outcomes of gestation—more of us would feel empowered to give a name to our complex feelings of loss, and less of us would feel as if these losses were somehow a fault of our own.

I think of all the change I've seen with my own eyes, and I well up and teem with hope when I imagine what it could mean for future generations. For our families. For my daughter. And my son. And their offspring. And onward.

• • •

These perspectives would not have arrived without my would-be daughter. I didn't know trauma firsthand, and heartbreak wasn't something I knew intimately, until I did. Until that inauspicious day: October 11, 2012. Declared the first International Day of the Girl, this was the day I lost mine. The day when cramping morphed into full-blown labor, and then my pregnancy precipitously ended. And then she was gone.

Invariably, this hit hard. It fractured an imagined dream, and so much more than that. Nothing had prepared me for this. Nothing. Nothing had prepared me for grief's labyrinthine complexity, its enduring nature, its serpentine permanence. Nothing. Nothing had previously educated me about the fact that grief can't be bypassed or replaced with platitudes, "positivity," or psalms. Grief commands attention. Grief demands time. And grief isn't to be tamed or tampered with. It is to be traveled, investigated, lavished, even. Studied. It doesn't give us much of a choice in the matter. It didn't for me, at least. In fact, the enormity of my loss lingers still, sometimes. How could it not? There are particular times of year when I feel that much more beholden to my grief. Or when it beckons. Shades of light, time of day, smells that waft: all things that can transport me back to that poignant period. October, most of all, tends to yield these feelings more than any other month, as the fall light escorts me back into the mood of that momentous experience.

On the anniversary of my loss, no matter the passage of time, every year, my heart burns. It stings to the core as I sift through the unbearable details. On a cellular level, I remember. The trauma of my loss remains palpable. In fact, nearly seven years later, I can still hear the D&C machine, loud with purpose, and the violent tugs that pulled my placenta from my body. I wonder if time will eventually evaporate this scene. I'm not so sure trauma works like that. Time helps ease the piercing intensity, but I don't necessarily believe that experiences this profound are meant to be forgotten, or that we can expect ourselves to disband grief altogether. Trauma, heartache, grief, and all the various other feelings that come along with these are, instead, integrated and remembered in no uncertain terms. We aren't necessarily meant to "move on" from these life-altering moments in a linear way. It is in fact normative, natural, and okay—more than okay—to sit in our grief, even when it feels as sharp as the day it first touched us. We aren't supposed to "move on," "be positive," or "push ahead" overnight. Perhaps there is something cathartic about feeling the pain, still—for when we don't feel it at all, we might worry we've lost all connection to that pregnancy. That somehow memory has faded. Perhaps we don't want to lose touch with this ache altogether because it is the last link to what we've lost.

A few months back, on my way home from work, I decided to take a detour, to swing by our first home—that window-clad house of ours tucked high in the Hollywood hills. The place we planned our destination wedding, brought Liev home from the hospital, where he took his first steps, and the place of my miscarriage. Less than a year after our loss, while I was very pregnant with Noa, we moved from the house where I lost Olive. Not because of the loss itself; simply because it was time. We had been search-ing for a while for a house with a flat yard and a one-level communal living space. This—our first nest—is the place where so much changed in an instant. The creation of life and its demise. And where I hemorrhaged after cutting the umbilical cord, and made a conscious effort to secure my survival. I parked in front of the place where life turned upside down, inside out at four months along. The light was almost exactly as it had been on that mid-October day: golden and decisive. It felt uncannily familiar. I wept briefly as I sank into remembering while looking up past the bamboo trees and into the rectangular window of the bathroom where she was born too soon. Olive. My love and compassion for all you women who feel this ache is fierce and enduring. May we persist in telling our important stories. My Olive, I think of you still. I'll think of you always.

## Epilogue

Dear Miscarriage,

Oh, how you have changed it all.

You give me no choice other than to dedicate much of my heart, energy, and love to you—to change how culture silences you, shrouds you in shame. You deserve serious and pointed attention.

I love you for helping me better understand suffering and resilience.

I've opened my heart fully to you.

I loathe you for the droplets of hopelessness interspersed. And the terrorizing anxiety that clung to my subsequent pregnancy.

But here's the thing, miscarriage: I've spent so much time getting to know you and my deepest self, my fundamental strength. I think—or more accurately, I know—it's time (long overdue, perhaps) that society spotlight you.

Highlight you. In neon.

No more shadowed, isolated grievers. No more mourners

wondering if they did something to deserve this. Nope. No more.

Just love.

Tenderness.

Honesty.

Hope.

And the ever-present proof that being human renders us vulnerable.

It's tough to say I love you, but I will say this: I love who you've helped me become.

With fortitude and a dedication to changing the dialogue around you,

Jessica

(a.k.a. @IHadaMiscarriage)

PS I'm sticking around. Don't think I'm going anywhere when it comes to you, miscarriage. You indelibly changed my emotional landscape, so you better believe I'm gonna do my best to evolve you, too.

# Notes

1. Katherine Hobson, "People Have Misconceptions about Miscarriage, and That Can Hurt," NPR, May 8, 2015, https://www.npr.org/sections/health-shots/2015/05/08/404913568/people-have-misconceptions-about-miscarriage-and-that-hurts.
2. Rebecca J. Mercier, Katherine Senter, Rachel Webster, and Amy Henderson Riley, "Instagram Users' Experiences of Miscarriage," *Obstetrics & Gynecology* 135, no. 1 (2020): 166–73, https://doi.org/10.1097/AOG.0000000000003621.
3. Jessica Farren, Maria Jalmbrant, Lieveke Ameye, et al., "Post-Traumatic Stress, Anxiety and Depression following Miscarriage or Ectopic Pregnancy: A Prospective Cohort Study," *BMJ Open* 6, no. 11 (2016), https://doi.org/10.1136/bmjopen-2016-011864.
4. Peter J. Fashing, Nga Nguyen, Tyler S. Barry, et al., "Death among Geladas (Theropithecus Gelada): A Broader Perspective on Mummified Infants and Primate Thanatology," *American Journal of Primatology* 73 no. 5 (2011): 405–409, https://doi.org/10.1002/ajp.20902.
5. Jessica Pierce, "Do Animals Experience Grief?" *Smithsonian Magazine*, August 24, 2018, https://www.smithsonianmag.com/science-nature/do-animals-experience-grief-180970124/; Barbara J. King, "When Animals Mourn: Seeing That

Grief Is Not Uniquely Human," NPR, April 11, 2013, https://www.npr.org/sections/13.7/2013/04/11/176620943/when-animals-mourn-seeing-that-grief-is-not-uniquely-human; Carl Safina, "The Depths of Animal Grief," PBS, July 8, 2015, https://www.pbs.org/wgbh/nova/article/animal-grief/.

6. Jerrold S. Meyer and Amanda F. Hamel, "Models of Stress in Nonhuman Primates and Their Relevance for Human Psychopathology and Endocrine Dysfunction," *ILAR Journal* 55 no. 2 (2014): 347–60, https://doi.org/10.1093/ilar/ilu023.

7. Rosanne Cecil, ed., *The Anthropology of Pregnancy Loss: Comparative Studies in Miscarriage, Stillbirth and Neo-natal Death* (Oxford, UK: Berg Publishers, 1996).

8. Cecil, *The Anthropology of Pregnancy Loss.*

9. Shannon Withycombe, "Happy Miscarriages: An Emotional History of Pregnancy Loss," Nursing Clio, November 12, 2015, https://nursingclio.org/2015/11/12/happy-miscarriages-an-emotional-history-of-pregnancy-loss/.

10. Shannon Withycombe, *Lost: Miscarriage in Nineteenth-Century America* (New Brunswick, NJ: Rutgers University Press, 2018).

11. Leslie J. Reagan, "From Hazard to Blessing to Tragedy: Representations of Miscarriage in Twentieth-Century America," *Feminist Studies* 29, no. 2 (2003): 356–78, https://www.jstor.org/stable/3178514.

12. Daniela Blei, "The History of Talking about Miscarriage," The Cut, April 23, 2018, https://www.thecut.com/2018/04/the-history-of-talking-about-miscarriage.html.

13. Jonah Bardos, Daniel Hercz, Jenna Friedenthal, et al., "A National Survey on Public Perceptions of Miscarriage," *Obstetrics & Gynecology* 125, no. 6 (2015): 1313–20, https://doi.org/10.1097/aog.0000000000000859.

14. Bardos, Hercz, Friedenthal, et al., "A National Survey on Public Perceptions of Miscarriage," 1313–20.

15. Raj Rai and Lesley Regan, "Recurrent Miscarriage," *The Lancet* 368, no. 9535 (2006): 601–11, https://doi.org/10.1016/S0140-6736(06)69204-0.

16. Bardos, Hercz, Friedenthal, et al., "A National Survey on Public Perceptions of Miscarriage," 1313–20.

17. Lynn Okura, "Brené Brown on Shame: 'It Cannot Survive Empathy,'" HuffPost, August 26, 2013, https://www.huffpost.com/entry/brene-brown-shame_n_3807115.

18. Hobson, "People Have Misconceptions about Miscarriage, and That Can Hurt."

19. *Merriam-Webster Online*, s.v. "karma," https://www.merriam-webster.com/dictionary/karma.

20. National Eating Disorders Association (NEDA), "People of Color and Eating Disorders," accessed July 8, 2020, https://www.nationaleatingdisorders.org/people-color-and-eating-disorders.

21. Hobson, "People Have Misconceptions about Miscarriage, and That Can Hurt"; Bardos, Hercz, Friedenthal, et al., "A National Survey on Public Perceptions of Miscarriage," 1313–20; Joshua Johnson, "What Does It Mean to Lose a Pregnancy?" June 5, 2019, in *1A*, produced by Paige Osburn, podcast, MP3 audio, https://www.npr.org/2019/06/05/730018199/what-does-it-mean-to-lose-a-pregnancy.

22. American Psychological Association, *What Is Postpartum Depression & Anxiety?* 2008, https://www.apa.org/pi/women/resources/reports/postpartum-depression.

23. Lexico, s.v. "healing," https://www.lexico.com/en/definition/healing.

24. Wikipedia, s.v. "Healing," accessed April 23, 2019, https://en.wikipedia.org/wiki/Healing.

# Acknowledgments

This book project came to fruition as a result of many dedicated, extraordinary people who believe in the transformative nature of storytelling. I am in awe of the unyielding support I received from my team throughout the process.

I am deeply grateful to my literary agent, Kate Johnson, for her unflinching belief in my voice. Ever since we connected, Kate's confidence in me has acted as a guiding light. Bringing rigor and levity to the process, her authenticity served as an ongoing reminder that the topic of pregnancy loss does in fact deserve to be normalized and deftly integrated into the zeitgeist.

Jamia Wilson and Lauren Rosemary Hook brought editorial brilliance and incisive wisdom to every aspect of the book-writing process. Their perspectives elevated the way I approached memoir writing and encouraged nuance and moxie as I made my way through the manifesto elements of the book as well. The Feminist Press team as a whole, especially Jisu Kim, Lucia Brown, and Rachel Page, have brought this book to life with passion, and to each and every one of them, I am thankful.

Sara Gaynes Levy's editorial cogency and insight helped shepherd me through this process. Editor turned friend, Sara was at once a cheerleader and a devoted editorial wizard. To her, I am thankful beyond measure. I also owe gratitude to Kay Friedman Holland and Laura Norkin for their ingenious acumen. They helped bring this book to new heights.

I credit Jessica Schneider, my obstetrician and dear friend, with providing exemplary medical care. Had she not walked me through what to do and how to do it over the phone that day, I likely would've been transported in an ambulance to the emergency room, flush with strangers, while giving birth to death. Instead, her professional prowess and astute emotional awareness allowed me to endure the loss of my daughter with dignity.

Valerie is a touchstone. An arbiter of compassion and revelatory understanding, she reminds me of my capacities and my humanity. I am humbled to know her.

My life partner and best friend, Jason, is the one who witnessed my unfolding and stood by me all the while. It is in the context of this relationship—and the trauma we endured—that I have come to understand that love can morph into even deeper iterations after surviving the unimaginable.

Thank you to my sweet Liev and Noa for making me a mother. Thank you for loving with abandon, for being teachers, and for redefining the word "love." Thank you for your sensitivity, sense of humor, soulfulness, and creativity. Thank you for being. Thank you for being you.

And to Olive, for making me a mother, too. For cracking me open and for requiring me to reconfigure emotionally in the deepest possible way—looking directly into the eyes of sheer vulnerability. For introducing me to the people and community I only met because I lost you. You are loved and remembered, not only by our family, but by countless women around the world who know our story and understand it too well.

I am grateful to my parents, and for the support of my sister and brother, for helping to lay the groundwork for becoming a storyteller. For instilling courage, an inner compass, and a joie de vivre.

Finally, thank you to all the people courageously sharing their stories and to those who opt to remain private about them.

## More Nonfiction from the Feminist Press

**Against Memoir:**
**Complaints, Confessions & Criticisms**
by Michelle Tea

**Black Dove: Mamá, Mi'jo, and Me**
by Ana Castillo

**But Some of Us Are Brave:**
**Black Women's Studies (Second Edition)**
edited by Akasha (Gloria T.) Hull, Patricia Bell Scott,
and Barbara Smith

**The Crunk Feminist Collection**
edited by Brittney C. Cooper, Susana M. Morris,
and Robin M. Boylorn

**The Echoing Ida Collection**
edited by Cynthia R. Greenlee, Kemi Alabi,
and Janna A. Zinzi

**Parenting for Liberation:**
**A Guide for Raising Black Children**
by Trina Greene Brown

**Radical Reproductive Justice:**
**Foundations, Theory, Practice, Critique**
edited by Loretta J. Ross, Lynn Roberts,
Erika Derkas, Whitney Peoples, and
Pamela Bridgewater Toure

**You Have the Right to Remain Fat**
by Virgie Tovar

**Your Art Will Save Your Life**
by Beth Pickens

**The Feminist Press** publishes books that ignite movements and social transformation. Celebrating our legacy, we lift up insurgent and marginalized voices from around the world to build a more just future.

See our complete list of books at
**feministpress.org**

**THE FEMINIST PRESS**
AT THE CITY UNIVERSITY OF NEW YORK
**NEW YORK CITY**